HEROES OF HISTORY

ERNEST SHACKLETON

Going South

Heroes of History

ERNEST SHACKLETON

Going South

JANET & GEOFF BENGE

Emerald Books
P.O. BOX 635, LYNNWOOD, WA 98046

Emerald Books are distributed through YWAM Publishing. For a full list of titles, including other great biographies, visit our website at www.emeraldbooks.com.

Ernest Shackleton: Going South

Published by Emerald Books
P.O. Box 635
Lynnwood, WA 98046

Library of Congress Cataloging-in-Publication Data

Names: Benge, Janet, 1958– author. | Benge, Geoff, 1954– author.
Title: Ernest Shackleton : going south / Janet and Geoff Benge.
Description: Lynnwood, WA : Emerald Books, [2017] | Series: Heroes of History | "Emerald Books are distributed through YWAM Publishing"—T.p. verso. | Includes bibliographical references. | Audience: Ages: 10–14.
Identifiers: LCCN 2016057806 (print) | LCCN 2016059539 (ebook) | ISBN 9781624860935 (paperback) | ISBN 9781624860959 (e-book)
Subjects: LCSH: Shackleton, Ernest Henry, Sir, 1874–1922—Juvenile literature. | British Antarctic Expedition (1907–1909) | Explorers—Great Britain—Biography—Juvenile literature. | Antarctica—Discovery and exploration—British—Juvenile literature.
Classification: LCC G875.S5 B44 2017 (print) | LCC G875.S5 (ebook) | DDC 919.8904092 [B] —dc23
LC record available at https://lccn.loc.gov/2016057806

Second printing 2024

Printed in the United States of America

HEROES OF HISTORY

Abraham Lincoln
Alan Shepard
Ben Carson
Benjamin Franklin
Benjamin Rush
Billy Graham
Captain John Smith
Christopher Columbus
Clara Barton
Davy Crockett
Daniel Boone
Douglas MacArthur
Dwight Eisenhower
Elizabeth Fry
Ernest Shackleton
Frederick Douglass
George Washington
George Washington Carver
Harriet Tubman
John Adams
Laura Ingalls Wilder
Louis Zamperini
Meriwether Lewis
Milton Hershey
Orville Wright
Ronald Reagan
Theodore Roosevelt
Thomas Edison
William Bradford
William Penn
William Wilberforce
Winston Churhill

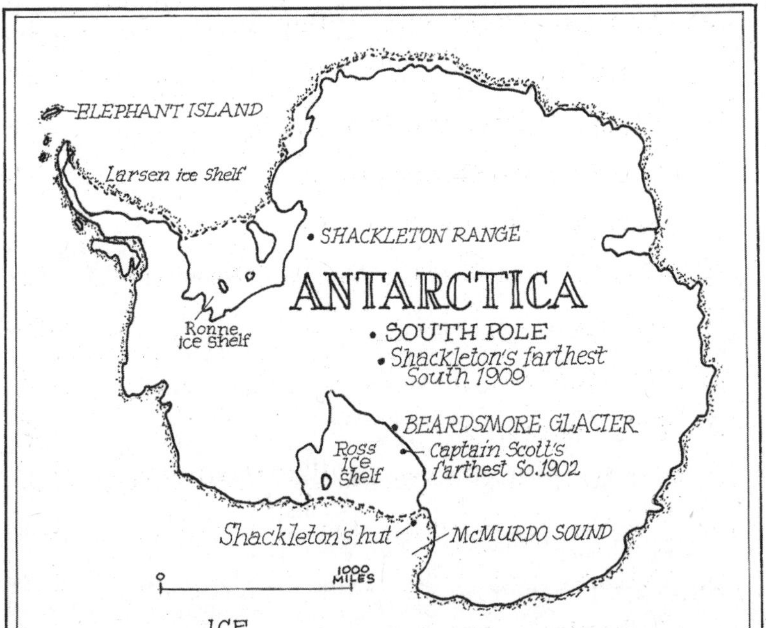
ELEPHANT ISLAND
Larsen ice Shelf
SHACKLETON RANGE
ANTARCTICA
Ronne Ice Shelf
SOUTH POLE
Shackleton's farthest South 1909
BEARDSMORE GLACIER
Ross Ice Shelf
Captain Scott's farthest So.1902
Shackleton's hut
McMURDO SOUND
0
1000 MILES
ICE

Contents

Chapter 1

Going South

Ernest Shackleton pulled his jacket tight around him against the bitter wind as the *Discovery* pitched and rolled in the angry sea. They had set sail from New Zealand nine days before, on Christmas Eve, and were now approaching the Antarctic Circle. Ernest stood staring down at the sea, studying the first chunk of floating pack ice they had seen. The ice hung low in the water, and the waves washed across it. Ernest knew that they would soon be encountering much more ice.

Sure enough, five days later, a vast white plain of pack ice spread before the ship. Beyond it, at the horizon, Ernest caught his first glimpse of something few others had ever seen—Antarctica. He could just make out the Admiralty Range of Victoria Land, bathed in golden light from the midnight sun. It was a sight he knew he would never forget.

On January 9, 1902, the *Discovery* dropped anchor off Cape Adare. A boat was lowered over the ship's side. Ernest was one of the men in it. He was about to set foot on the frozen continent for the first time. The bottom of the boat scraped to a stop on a shingle beach crowded with thousands of Adélie penguins. As the birds squawked around him, Ernest studied the frozen, desolate scene. This had to be one of the most inhospitable places on earth, yet something about it drew him to this frozen land, something he couldn't explain.

As a boy at Kilkea House back in Ireland, Ernest had spent hundreds of hours in his make-believe ship on the lawn, but never in all those imagined journeys had he dreamed of going south on an adventure like this.

Chapter 2

Dreams of Adventure

Ernest Shackleton sat by his bedroom window staring out at the rolling farmland. "It's going to be very exciting," his mother said. "There'll be many things to see and do in Dublin. There's the zoo and the double-decker streetcars to ride . . ."

"I know," Ernest said. "Father's told me all about it. He says he'll take me down to the docks too."

"There," his mother smiled, tousling his hair, "what six-year-old boy wouldn't love to see the tall ships coming and going all over the world?"

Ernest nodded. He knew they had to go. His father, thirty-three-year-old Henry Shackleton, was returning to Trinity College in Dublin to study to become a doctor. He already had a degree in arts from the college. When Ernest asked why he needed to become a doctor, his father said it was complicated. It had something to do with changing Irish land-ownership laws and the need to make enough money to feed a growing family.

Ernest was anxious about moving thirty-five miles northeast, away from the lush Irish countryside and into the city. He especially didn't like the idea of leaving his special place on the lawn—the huge fallen tree trunk he imagined to be a ship. From the bow of his ship he had commanded many imaginary voyages to India and China, encountering pirates and deserted islands along the way.

The next day a coach arrived at the house for the family. Ernest ran to his make-believe ship to watch the proceedings. His younger brother, four-year-old Frank, trailed behind asking questions. Most of them were easy to answer. No, the Shackleton family wouldn't be coming back to Kilkea House in County Kildare to live. They didn't own the place. They leased it. Yes, their four sisters were coming too, and Nanny. And no, he didn't know if there was a big tree trunk on the lawn of their new house in Dublin, but he hoped so.

Ernest watched his mother carry baby Eleanor to the coach. Nanny followed with Amy and Ethel. His older sister, eight-year-old Gertrude, walked behind carrying extra clothes for the little ones.

"Ernest, Frank, it's time to go," Ernest's mother called. Frank ran to the coach, but Ernest hesitated. He looked up at the second-floor window of the room where he was born on February 15, 1874. He had never lived anywhere else and loved his life as an Anglo-Irish farmer's son. It was hard to imagine a different life. To cheer himself up, Ernest hummed his favorite song:

> Twinkle, twinkle, little star,
> How I wonder what you are
> Up above the world so high
> Like a diamond in the sky . . .

As he hummed, he thought of all the times he had lain on his "ship" watching the sun set over Mullaghcreelan Hill and the stars appear in the night sky.

"Ernest, come here," Henrietta Shackleton called again.

This time he jumped down and raced to his mother. He couldn't put it off any longer. It was time to leave.

The coach, pulled by four horses, rolled through the countryside. It was early autumn, and the hedgerows were covered with ripe blackberries, which Ernest would have loved to eat. Instead he peered out the window as the driver reached the crossroad and turned northward toward Ballitore. He knew the road well. He had often traveled it to visit relatives. Six miles in the other direction lay Castledermot, where his grandmother on his mother's side lived. Her family had lived in Ireland since before the twelfth century, while his father's family had settled there over 150 years before. Ernest knew the story well. His ancestor, Abraham Shackleton, was a Quaker who moved from his home in Yorkshire, England, to Ballitore to tutor Quaker children. He had started a school that became one of the best boys boarding schools in Ireland. Even so, Ernest felt sorry for the boys who went there. They arrived from all over the world at five years old, and some never saw their parents again until graduation at eighteen years of age. Ernest loved his parents, and it was hard to imagine not seeing them each day, much less being without them for thirteen years.

After a day's travel, the coach pulled into a narrow street lined with a terrace of identical two-story red brick houses.

"Here we are, number 35 Marlborough Road," Henrietta told her children. "Remember that, so that if you ever get lost, you can tell someone where you live, and they will point you homeward."

Ernest noted the address. He loved roaming around the fields in Kilkea and was sure he would love exploring Dublin on his own as well. Soon everyone settled into a new routine. His father studied or tended the roses in the garden. When the weather was good, Nanny took the children for walks in St. Stephen's Green, while Ernest's mother rested. She had told Ernest that another baby was on the way. Although he hoped for a brother, it was another girl, who was named Clara.

Soon after they arrived, Ernest's parents hired a governess to teach their eldest son to read and write. Each day Ernest had lessons at home with the governess. As part of the boy's education, his father sometimes came to the nursery to talk about what was happening in the world. It was difficult for Ernest to understand what made the Irish want their country to be independent from Great Britain.

All he knew was that his father thought it a good idea.

On May 6, 1882, two years after arriving in Dublin, Ernest learned just how brutal the desire for independence could be. On that day, two prominent British politicians, Thomas Burke and Lord Cavendish, the newly appointed chief secretary for Ireland, were stabbed to death at Phoenix Park in broad daylight. The attackers were members of the Irish National Invincibles, a radical group that wanted the British out of Ireland.

Given the unrest, Henry Shackleton warned his children against participating in large gatherings, such as parades. Rebel processions often marched with brass bands, and Ernest's father specifically forbade Ernest from going to the parades. The events were too dangerous to be around. This was frustrating for Ernest, who loved crowds and pomp and ceremony. Instead, he contented himself with funeral processions. Whenever he heard a procession passing down the street, he would run outside and follow it. His mother teased him about this, but Ernest didn't care. He joined right in, pretending he was mourning with the others in the procession.

As Ernest studied under the governess, his reading improved, and he discovered he loved poetry. Soon he was learning poems by heart. He also loved having adventures outside. Once he dug a hole in the garden, convinced that if he went deep enough he would come out in Australia. Another time, desperately wanting to find buried treasure, he borrowed his mother's ruby ring and buried it in the ground. Ernest then invited Nanny to watch him dig it up.

The Shackleton family continued to grow. Two more babies arrived in quick succession. Much to Ernest's disappointment, they were both girls: Helen and Kathleen. This gave him a total of seven sisters. Ernest's father continued studying at Trinity College, and in June 1884 he graduated with double degrees: a master's in medicine and a master's in surgery. Given the political turmoil surrounding independence in Ireland, Dr. Henry Shackleton decided to move his family of seven girls and two boys to England.

Ernest ran up the gangplank of the *Banchee,* the ship that would take them from Kingstown across the Irish Sea to Holyhead in Wales. He had always enjoyed it when his father took him to watch ships come and go, and now he was going to sail on one. At last his life had some adventure! He had just finished reading *Life with the Esquimaux* by Charles Francis Hall, an American polar explorer who went in search of Sir John Franklin's lost Arctic expedition of 1847. In the course of doing so, the explorer spent time living with the local Eskimos. Everything about the story captivated Ernest's imagination, and he decided that once he got to England, he would read all he could about polar explorers. In contrast to Hall's voyage, the Shackleton trip across the Irish Sea was short and uneventful, but Ernest knew that one day he would go much farther.

In England the Shackleton family moved into a house in South Croydon, a suburb of London, but things didn't go well there. Ernest's father could not find enough patients, and so money was short. Within months the family moved to Sydenham, seven miles closer to London, and rented Aberdeen House, on West Hill. Ernest's room was next to the bell tower on Saint Bartholomew's Church. Ernest loved hearing the bells reverberate through the house. It was a much better location for his father, who built a thriving medical practice as the family settled into a new routine.

Part of the new routine included Ernest going to school for the first time. He was enrolled at Fir Lodge Preparatory School and began attending classes after Christmas 1886, just before his thirteenth birthday. Ernest was sure he knew what to expect. After all, he had read every edition of the *Boy's Own Paper*, a weekly magazine filled with stories for boys. Many of those stories were set in English schools. He dreamed of finding hidden tunnels, chasing black adders off the cricket pitch, and uncovering plots to kidnap teachers.

The reality Ernest encountered was quite different. Ernest soon discovered that Fir Lodge was a dame school. Located just a few minutes' walk from his home, the school was run by a humorless old schoolmarm named Miss Higgins. She was partly deaf and used an ear trumpet to aid her hearing. She soon surprised Ernest by how well she kept an eye on all the boys.

Because the Shackletons were Irish, every time Ernest opened his mouth at school, he reminded his classmates of the fact. The boys teased him about his thick accent and nicknamed him Mickey after St. Michael, an Irish saint. Sometimes Ernest fought back against the teasing with his fists, earning himself a reputation as a good fighter.

Apart from schoolyard fighting, there were no adventures to be had at Fir Lodge Preparatory School for Ernest, just a lot of grammar and algebra. It didn't help that he didn't like to study and was content with his place near the bottom of the class. Despite his lack of effort, two years later Ernest was accepted as a day boy at Dulwich College in southeast London. Dulwich was an old college, established in 1619, and promised a solid high school education for the modest sum of fifteen pounds per year.

At Dulwich, Ernest's grades didn't improve. His school reports contained comments from his teachers that were all variations of the same theme: "He has not yet fully exerted himself." "Wants waking up, is rather listless." "Not a very clear-headed boy yet." "Often sinks into idleness." "Must remember the importance of accuracy." But most of the teachers went on to say that with increased effort in his schoolwork he might do well.

Henry Shackleton talked to Ernest about studying harder and becoming a doctor, but Ernest couldn't imagine himself going to the same surgery every day, year after year, to talk to sick people. He didn't know what he wanted to be when he left school, but he knew it would include travel and adventure.

Henrietta Shackleton gave birth to another daughter, whom they named Gladys. There were now ten children in the Shackleton home, eight girls and two boys. Soon after Gladys's birth, Ernest's mother became ill. No one knew what the illness was, but it became difficult for Henrietta to get out of bed and move around. At forty-two years of age, she had to give up her role as an active mother and retire to bed upstairs. Ernest's grandmother, Caroline Gavan, came from Ireland to help with the smallest children, while the older girls took over many of the household tasks. Ernest missed his mother's cheerful presence downstairs.

To Ernest, studying at Dulwich College was just as boring as it was at Fir Lodge, and more so now that Greek and Latin were added to his curriculum. He also had to take part in various school sports. He did well in boxing and gymnastics but not so well in cricket and rugby.

Walking the mile to school and back again each day, Ernest planned ways to escape the predictable life he led. He still kept in touch with three boys from Fir Lodge Preparatory School: Arthur "Griff" Griffith, Ned Sleap, and Christol Kay. They attended different schools now, and they were all bored studying. They made a pact to start skipping classes and meet in the gully of Silverdale Woods.

The first time the boys met, each one brought something to do. Ernest found an old box in the garden that was soon deposited in the gully and filled with a revolver and ammunition, a flute, a concertina, and a large model boat. From then on the boys spent as much time as possible at their hideout, including some Saturdays. In winter they lit a fire and roasted chestnuts. Sometimes the boys drank cooking sherry, but Ernest refused to have any. He belonged to the Band of Hope, a children's organization designed to bring attention to the perils of drinking alcohol.

In the box at the gully, Ernest also kept some copies of his *Boy's Own Paper* and read seagoing adventures aloud to the other boys. He also loved reciting adventure poems. His favorite was *The Wreck of the Hesperus*, all eighty-eight lines of it. Griff brought along a ball of string, and the boys rigged and rerigged the model ship. All four boys talked about their dream of a career at sea. They eventually tired of sitting in Silverdale Woods for long periods of time and needed a more exciting adventure. Fifteen-year-old Ernest Shackleton knew just what it should be—it was time for them to run away to sea together.

Chapter 3

To Sea

On a bright spring morning, Ernest, Griff, and Christol boarded the 9:30 train for London Bridge Station. Ned was unable to join them. Each boy carried a small pack containing a change of clothes, cheese, and bread. The boys were off to join a ship—any ship—for an adventure at sea. From London Bridge Station they walked the short distance to the docks on the Thames River. High-masted schooners and modern steamships were moored along the docks, busily loading and unloading cargo. The boys wandered around for an hour watching all the activity around them until they plucked up the courage to join a line of men beside a large steamer. A man in line told Ernest the ship was bound for the South Seas and the chief steward was taking applications for stewards to serve on board. The three boys waited patiently. Slowly they moved up the gangplank onto the ship. When they made it to the chief steward, the man asked them, "An' what can I do for you, lads?"

"We've come to enlist," Ernest said.

"You have, have you?" the steward replied. "And how old might you be?"

"I'm fifteen," Ernest answered.

"And do you have parents?"

"Yes, sir."

"And they know you're here?" the chief steward asked.

"No, sir," Ernest said, and pointing at Griff and Christol, he added, "It's us that want to go to sea."

The chief steward chuckled. "Many a boy wants to go to sea, but you'll all be missed for sure. I can't risk signing up a boy with a home to go back to. Run along before you get into trouble." He motioned for the next man to step forward.

The three boys walked glumly down the gangplank. They wandered around the docks and made a few other job inquiries, but the response was always the same. Ernest concluded that they all looked too respectable to get a job on a ship without their parents' permission.

The adventure wasn't going the way they planned, but the boys were determined to do something exciting. Instead of returning home, they spent the night in an empty boxcar on a siding at London Bridge Station. After an uncomfortable night, they wandered the docks once more, discussing ships' rigging and guessing the tonnage of various vessels. As night fell, they caught the train back to Sydenham.

Ernest's parents were relieved when their son returned home. His father was not surprised that he had tried to run away to sea. Being a practical man, he agreed to let Ernest go to sea on two conditions. First, he must finish the next term at Dulwich College and show improvement in his studies. And second, they had to find a kind, respectable captain to sign Ernest onto his crew.

Joining the Royal Navy was not an option. It cost seventy pounds a year to be a crew member on the cadet training ship, more than Ernest's father could afford. Instead, Henry Shackleton turned to his cousin, the Reverend Charles Woosnam, for help. Charles lived in Liverpool and ran the Mersey Mission to Seamen. He soon reported good news. He had found a position for Ernest aboard the *Hoghton Tower*, an old-style, 1,600-ton, fully rigged sailing ship that hauled cargo around the world. The captain was Charles's friend and did not tolerate excessive drunkenness or other bad behavior aboard his ship. Ernest would be a ship's boy, the lowest-ranked and lowest-paid crew member aboard, earning one shilling a month. But none of this mattered to him. It was Ernest's chance to head out into the open ocean and experience real adventure. If all went well, after a year, Ernest could become an apprentice sailor. His father told him he was happy with the arrangement. Ernest could come home again after a year if he found seagoing life too difficult.

Of course, to take up the position, Ernest had to complete the first requirement his father had laid down: he had to finish his term at Dulwich College and improve his grades. He concentrated on his schoolwork as never before, and the results showed it. From being bottom in his class of twenty-five boys, he pulled himself up to third in mathematics and chemistry and second in history and literature. This was enough to satisfy his father.

On April 2, 1890, Ernest walked home from Dulwich College for the last time. He felt invigorated. School was behind him, and at sixteen years of age, he was ready to embrace the rest of his life. Because Ernest's mother was still bedridden, Gertrude helped him pack his sea chest. The old brown chest had belonged to Ernest's mother's parents. Before Henrietta was born, Ernest's grandfather, Henry John Gavan, was appointed inspector general of police in Ceylon. In 1844 he and his wife sailed from Falmouth on their way to Ceylon. But the ship ran into a fierce storm and after ten days turned back. Ernest's grandparents disembarked and could not face getting back on board. Instead, the sea chest was unpacked and over time became the grandchildren's toy box. Now the chest was off to sea again. Ernest hoped he would have better luck on the *Hoghton Tower* than his grandparents had when they set sail.

On Saturday, April 19, 1890, everything was packed, and Ernest boarded the train north to Liverpool. As the train wound through the English countryside, Ernest thought of the boys still studying back in school and how lucky he was to have an understanding father who had arranged all of this for him.

Ten days later Ernest stood proudly on the deck of the North-Western Shipping Company's *Hoghton*

Tower. The ship was towed down the Mersey River and into the Irish Sea, bound for Valparaíso, Chile. On the way the sailors would travel through some of the roughest ocean in the world rounding Cape Horn.

The ship's cargo was hay. On the return voyage, the ship would carry a load of sodium nitrate. By now, sailing ships were giving way to steam-powered vessels. The *Hoghton Tower* was a dying breed often used for long hauls of agricultural cargo.

For the first week the sea was calm and the weather sunny. Ernest felt mildly seasick but not enough to send him to his bunk. He quickly learned how to do the most menial jobs on board and enthusiastically polished the brass, scrubbed the decks, and lugged buckets of food from the galley to the forecastle, or fo'c'sle, where the ordinary seamen ate.

A ship's boy was also expected to learn the ropes so that he could climb the rigging and trim the sails. Ernest discovered that learning the ropes was a complex job. The *Hoghton Tower* was a three-masted schooner. The bosun explained that in fact there were only nine "ropes" aboard. Everything else was referred to as a "line." As they walked around the ship together, the bosun pointed out halyards, tacks, sheets, buntlines, downhauls, outhauls, spilling lines, leech lines, clew lines, reef tackles, bowlines, guys, and clew garnets. Ernest's job was to learn not only the names of the 240 lines but also what each one did and where it was. It was a daunting task, but Ernest kept at it. If he could memorize lines of poetry to recite, he knew he could certainly learn the names of the lines and their function.

Each night Ernest slept well. In fact he had never before been so exhausted at the end of a day. He enjoyed the challenge of learning new things and the excitement of what might lie ahead. And just as his father's cousin had said, Captain Partridge was a kind man. He invited Ernest and the apprentices to his cabin each Sunday night for a round of hymn singing and Bible reading. The captain accompanied the singing with his flute, causing Ernest, who had a good ear for music, to wince at the notes coming from the instrument.

During the first weeks of the voyage, the weather was perfect for sailing. The *Hoghton Tower* cut through the ocean at a fast clip, even compared to a steamer. One day it covered three hundred miles. As the miles rolled by, Ernest recorded a series of firsts for him in his letters home. He had seen his first dead whale, a school of flying fish, a shark, and old King Neptune himself for the crossing of the equator. This was something he had read about, so he knew what lay ahead. He and the new apprentices were covered with sticky tar, and their heads were shaved. Then, as the ship crossed the equator, each boy was dunked in a tank, thus joining the fellowship of sailors who had passed from one hemisphere to the other. Captain Partridge made sure that things didn't get out of hand. As Ernest wrote about these things, he felt a pang of homesickness thinking about how much Griff, Ned, and Christol would enjoy them.

The good weather broke in June, and Ernest woke to the violent pitching and rolling of the ship along with the dripping of water in his cabin. On deck he was ordered into the rigging to help reef the sails. It was a daunting task in a storm, but Ernest climbed up, one foot after the other, holding onto the rigging tightly. Adrenaline coursed through his body as he realized that this was what real danger felt like, and he knew he was made for the challenge.

Following the buffeting from the storm, the *Hoghton Tower* closed in on Cape Horn at the southern tip of South America. The temperature plunged, and the closer the ship got to Cape Horn, the fiercer the storm became. The wind tore several sails from the yardarms and caused some of the lighter spars to crash to the deck. The second mate, who was in charge of Ernest, got caught under one of the falling spars, and his thigh was broken. Ernest narrowly escaped when an iron tackle plummeted to the deck. He was shaken but unhurt. Two of the ship's boats were washed off the deck.

It was the depth of winter in the Southern Hemisphere as they rounded Cape Horn. Ernest had never been so cold in his life as when he had to climb aloft to check the lines. The *Hoghton Tower* would climb mountainous waves and then drop heavily into the trough between them, sending a deluge of freezing sea spray high into the air, drenching him.

The ship made it safely around Cape Horn and sailed into the Pacific Ocean. Ernest was sure that no one aboard was happier than he when they reached Valparaíso in the middle of August. By then he had been at sea fifteen weeks and was glad to be invited to visit the British consul with Captain Partridge. It was wonderful to enjoy a meal of fresh vegetables, roast beef, and an array of tropical desserts.

For the next six weeks the *Hoghton Tower* remained docked in Valparaíso while her galley was restocked and the spars, sails, and boats lost in the storm were replaced. After the six weeks, she sailed on up the coast of Chile to Iquique. Because the town had no docks, the *Hoghton Tower* anchored offshore. At Iquique her cargo of hay was unloaded to a fleet of smaller boats called lighters that ferried it ashore. When the ship's hold was emptied, a cargo of sodium nitrate was loaded aboard, carried to the ship from the beach on the lighters. The mineral, a fine, white powder, was mined in the sparse hills behind the town. The ship lay at anchor off Iquique for six weeks until all the sacks of white gold, as the sodium nitrate was referred to, were loaded aboard.

Ernest soon discovered that loading the sacks into the hold from the lighters was backbreaking work. The sacks were hauled up on deck in nets, from where the crew, including Ernest, formed a chain to manhandle the sacks into the hold. The work was dirty, tiring, and dangerous. To make matters worse, the crew couldn't leave the ship and go ashore in the evenings. Captain Partridge told them it was too dangerous ashore. Stories abounded of sailors who had been robbed and beaten, and some sailors had never returned to their ships.

In the six weeks the *Hoghton Tower* lay at anchor off Iquique, Ernest began wondering why he had chosen a life at sea. Perhaps his father was right that he should look for a more respectable job on land. His gloomy mood was intensified on the last day at Iquique, when Ernest slid down a loosely tied rope to a lighter boat and fell into the sea. Thankfully, someone saw him, and he was quickly rescued, embarrassed but none the worse for the dunking.

Ernest was happy when the *Hoghton Tower* weighed anchor on December 1, 1890, and sailed away. The ship sailed south down the coast of Chile and back around Cape Horn. The *Hoghton Tower* made good time, and four months after leaving Iquique, she docked at Falmouth, England, to take on more food and water and to learn the final destination for the cargo. The sodium nitrate was bound for Hamburg, Germany. After a hearty meal of eggs and sausages, Ernest was back aboard ship as she headed out for Germany.

At the end of April the *Hoghton Tower* was towed back up the Mersey and docked in Liverpool. Ernest was home at last, almost exactly a year after embarking on his sailing adventure. Captain Partridge told Ernest he had filled out the paperwork for him to become an apprentice if that was what he wanted. Later Ernest learned that the captain had reported back to Charles Woosnam that he was "the most pigheaded, obstinate boy I have ever come across; yet there is no real fault to find with him, and he can do his work right well."

Seventeen-year-old Ernest took the train back to Sydenham. In the year he had been away, he felt he had grown five years. He wondered how he would fit in at home. When he arrived, his eight sisters mobbed him. For once in his life Ernest was speechless! He soon got back to his old, jovial self and played all sorts of tricks on the girls. At their first dinner he pretended he had forgotten how to eat in a civilized way, staring quizzically at his knife and fork. During the meal he ate with his hands and dipped his fingers in his water. The older sisters soon caught on and laughed, but some of the younger ones appeared to believe his acting and thought their brother really had forgotten how to be an Englishman.

Once the frivolities were over, Ernest had a serious decision to make. Would he go back to sea as an apprentice? As he looked back on the experience as a ship's boy, he felt unsure. Going to sea hadn't been quite the adventure he had hoped. In fact, the little of South America he saw was unglamorous, and he had worked harder than he imagined possible. Still, if he did go back and sign on for a three-year apprenticeship, by the time he was twenty-one he would be an officer in the merchant marine, the first step on the journey to becoming a captain. But was that what he wanted?

Chapter 4

Apprenticeship on the High Seas

In mid-June 1891, after six weeks at home, Ernest watched his father sign the apprenticeship papers binding him to the North-Western Shipping Company for three years. During that time, he would work and study to become a ship's officer. It hadn't been an easy decision for Ernest. He was aware that life at sea was hard, dangerous, and not nearly as glamorous as schoolboys thought it was. As he watched the contract being signed, he thought of the Shackleton family motto: *Fortitudine Vincimus*, "By endurance we conquer." He felt proud to be stepping up to the hardships awaiting him rather than shrinking from them.

This time Ernest had a better idea of what to pack. He included a small brown teapot and a spirit stove for making his own tea. The brewed tea served on the *Hoghton Tower* was so weak that he decided to make his own in the future. Half of his sea chest was filled with books, all sorts of books. He had his Bible and a daily Christian meditation, *Vanity Fair,* Robert Browning's poetry, and several books on world history, including all three volumes of John Motley's *Rise of the Dutch Republic.*

Ernest was reassigned to the *Hoghton Tower*, though this time under the command of a new, sterner captain, Robert Robinson. Eight apprentices were aboard, and as Ernest settled into their cabin, he learned that only two of them had been at sea longer than he. He smiled to himself. This time he would not be the lowest in the pecking order, getting the most menial jobs.

The *Hoghton Tower* sailed from Cardiff, Wales, on June 25, 1891, her hold filled with sacks of briquettes, a fuel made from a mixture of coal and pitch. Once again she was bound for Iquique, Chile, and once again the voyage started off with calm seas and fair winds. But that all changed when the ship reached Cape Horn. Ernest hardly imagined it possible, but the storms were more ferocious than the first time he had rounded the cape. The crew battled stiff winds and huge waves for nearly a month. Because the conditions were too rough to use the galley, the crew, from the captain to the newest apprentice, ate cold biscuits and dried meat meal after meal. Before long, one officer and eight crewmen were disabled by accidents, and what was worse, one sailor was washed overboard and could not be rescued.

Being young and fit, Ernest fared better than most of the crew, though the constant chafing of wet clothes and resting on a sodden bunk began wearing on his health as the weeks passed.

In the middle of October, after fighting her way through storm after storm, the *Hoghton Tower* dropped anchor off Iquique. The place was just as desolate as the year before, and as the sailors moved the first sacks of briquettes up onto the deck, Ernest wished they were at sea again. He wasn't sure why, but for some reason he felt more homesick this time than on the previous voyage. He thought about his apprenticeship and prayed that the years would go by fast.

It was nearly Christmas when the ship was ready to sail again. Once more her hold was filled with sacks of white gold—sodium nitrate—all loaded by hand.

In May 1892 the *Hoghton Tower* reached the Mersey and docked at Liverpool. Ernest had a break before the ship sailed again. He took the train to London, sending a telegraph before leaving to let his family know he was coming. When he arrived in Sydenham, his sisters were prepared for him. Every window and doorway in the house was festooned with bunting for his homecoming. His sisters smothered him with hugs, and when he mentioned the bunting, they giggled and told him that passersby had asked what public holiday they were celebrating. Ernest told them never to make such a fuss over him again, but from the look on their faces, he knew they would.

Ernest spent a month visiting old friends, watching the Dulwich College cricket team play, taking in the sights of London, and willingly inspecting his father's prize roses. He also selected a bag of new books to take with him. His friends teased him, noting that the boy who did everything he could to leave school now took books with him wherever he went.

Before Ernest knew it, he was back aboard the *Hoghton Tower,* this time headed for Madras, India, with a cargo of salt. As they set sail, Ernest noted that many of the sailors on this trip were tougher than those on the previous voyage. As he heard their stories, his alarm grew. He wrote to a school friend, "The characters you meet with are the most mixed kinds, for instance in the watch I am in viz.:—the starboard one; there is an American who had to flee his country for killing a coloured man. . . . Only the other day I saw a man stab another with a knife in the thigh right up to the handle."

Ernest tried to get along with everyone aboard and spent his spare hours alone reading books and writing letters.

Two months into the voyage, after passing the Cape of Good Hope at the bottom of Africa, Ernest was at the helm when a terrific storm appeared on the horizon and whipped toward them. The sky grew black and the ocean churned. There wasn't time to shorten the sail before the storm was upon them. Ernest battled to hold the wheel steady as lightning flashed around the ship. He heard a mighty rip and looked up to see the sails being stripped off the mast. Without sails the ship began to turn broadside to the wind. Huge waves flooded across the decks, deluged the cabins below, and threatened to swamp them completely.

When the first mate took over for Ernest, there was little that either of them could do. Ernest was ordered below deck as the storm raged into the night. He sat on a barrel surrounded by filthy seawater and looked around. Most of the other sailors were with him, and Ernest knew that they were just as scared as he was, since not one of them swore or cursed. They all sat quietly, as if they had already resigned themselves to drowning.

The dawn broke and the *Hoghton Tower* was still afloat. As the day went on, the sea calmed. Ernest helped get another set of sails up from below, and the ship was rerigged. It was hard work, but Ernest was grateful to be alive. Despite the lashing of the waves, the ship's cargo was still dry and intact.

India had sounded to Ernest like a glamorous destination, but by the time he arrived in Madras he was exhausted and feeling depressed. Instead of being able to explore the colorful city, he was stuck in the ship's hold repacking thousands of pounds of salt into smaller bags. It was about as far from any scene in a *Boy's Own Paper* story as he could imagine.

Early in the new year 1893 the *Hoghton Tower* moved some distance up the coast to False Point, where they picked up a cargo of rice bound for Mauritius. If Ernest thought salt was bad, taking on the rice was worse. The twenty-six hundred bags, each weighing 170 pounds, had to be passed over the railing of the ship and then passed man to man down into the hold. Before long, Ernest's hands were raw and too cut up to write properly.

Things went from bad to worse when they arrived at Port Louis in Mauritius. By then most of the crew were sick with diarrhea and vomiting, and Ernest was one of the sickest. He was still recovering three months later when the *Hoghton Tower* sailed into Newcastle, New South Wales, Australia, at the end of April. The ship stayed at Newcastle for six weeks loading coal before heading for Chile.

About halfway across the Pacific, one of the sailors died suddenly. His body was laid out in the saloon, and the apprentices took turns through the night keeping the rats off it. The man was buried at sea the following morning. By now Ernest was aware that sailors were among the most superstitious people on earth. Everything seemed to be an omen for good or bad. A dead sailor was a particularly bad omen, and the crew left the short funeral ceremony with a sense of impending doom.

Ernest returned to his lookout on the forequarter of the ship. He had been there only ten minutes when it began to rain. He put on his oilskin jacket, pants, and hat and watched as the second mate began to take in the light sails. Suddenly, forked lightning lit up the ship, and a whirlwind struck near Ernest. His hat flew off, and he crawled down the deck after it.

Ernest heard a tearing, crashing sound above him. As he instinctively crawled windward, he heard an enormous crash. He looked to see the fore royal mast, the topgallant mast, and the topmast all topple overboard. The heavy wire stays anchoring them to the deck whipped up about thirty feet into the air. They then lashed across the deck, right where Ernest had been standing before he lost his hat. Ernest shuddered. He knew that the whiplashing wires could slice through a man like butter.

With the next flash of lightning Ernest could see that the mainmast and yard had also gone overboard. All of the fallen masts were now tangled in a web of wires and rope lines off the starboard side. And every wave carried them back toward the ship like battering rams. If one of the masts hit the ship, it could easily punch a hole right through her wooden hull.

Once the storm passed, it took four days to clear the wreckage. No one got much sleep. At last the battered ship, minus most of her masts and sails, got under way, sailing on toward Chile. Ernest was glad to be alive, though in the storm his cherished sea chest that had belonged to his grandfather had been smashed to pieces below deck and everything inside it was soaked. He hated throwing the remains of the chest overboard, but the chest was beyond repair.

The *Hoghton Tower* arrived off Chile two months after leaving Australia and discharged some of its cargo of coal at Talcahuano before sailing north to Tocopilla. The sailors stayed there two months repairing the ship, unloading the remainder of the coal, and reloading with sodium nitrate. During this time many crew members, including Ernest, were still sick and depressed. But Ernest was determined to stick things out, even when Captain Robinson had a breakdown, resigned his command, and took a steamer back to England.

The ship's luck did not improve with a new captain. At the beginning of December, the ship sailed for Queenstown, Ireland, but it struck another storm and had to turn back when her newly replaced masts were ripped off.

Ernest spent the first few months of 1894 in Valparaíso as the *Hoghton Tower* underwent repairs. At the end of June 1894 the ship at last arrived in Queenstown. Ernest was back in Ireland after being away for ten years. He drank in the sights of the country of his birth: the neat rows of houses on the waterfront, with Saint Colman's Cathedral towering behind them all. He also visited some relatives living nearby.

A month later, after sailing to Dunkirk, France, to unload the cargo of sodium nitrate, the two-year voyage that had taken Ernest around the world came to an end. Once more, bunting hung from every window and door when Ernest returned to his family at Aberdeen House in Sydenham.

The three years of Ernest's apprenticeship were over. All that remained for Ernest was to pass the Board of Trade exams, which would qualify him to be a second officer. He easily passed them and began making plans for the next phase of his life. He had no desire to be an officer on another sailing ship. The ships were old, physically demanding, and dangerous. It was time for him to find a steamship.

In fall 1894 Ernest visited an old school friend, Owen Burne. Owen ran a wine-importing business, and Ernest figured if anyone knew the best shipping line to join, it would be his old school friend. Owen took him to visit the Welsh Shire Line office, where, after some introductions, Ernest was offered a job as fourth officer on one of their ships. Even though he had hoped to be a third officer, he went to check out the *Monmouthshire*. Ernest found the fourth mate's quarters cramped and right next to the engine. "I'll sign on only if you give me the job as third officer," he told the shipping line official. The official laughed and nodded. "All right. Sometimes you get what you ask for, lad," he said. "The third mate's job is yours."

Once again Ernest Shackleton went home to pack his belongings and say farewell to his family.

Chapter 5

In the Merchant Marine

On November 15, 1894, Ernest strolled along the dock on the Thames River. He thought back five and a half years to when he, Griff, and Christol begged to be signed on as stewards to a vessel berthed at the same dock. Now he was third officer on a ship, and both Griff and Christol were also at sea.

The *Monmouthshire* bustled with activity as Ernest stepped aboard. She was bound for China and Japan. Where she went after that depended on what cargo they picked up there. For the first time in his seafaring career, Ernest would be working on a ship that also carried passengers. He was excited about the possibility of meeting a wider range of interesting people while at sea.

The 1,900-ton *Monmouthshire* was very different from the *Hoghton Tower*. The ship was a steel-hulled steamer fitted with a powerful three-cylinder triple expansion steam engine. She was 344 feet long and 40 feet wide and much more stable and comfortable. Unlike a sailing ship, the *Monmouthshire* didn't pitch and roll at the mercy of the wind. In a storm, instead of having to furl the sails, the steam engines kept powering the vessel forward. About the only thing that took Ernest a while to adjust to was the constant noise and throb of the steam engine.

The voyage got off to a good start. Ernest liked the ship's master, Captain Evans, and made many friends among the crew and passengers. Unlike most officers, Ernest mixed with anyone who interested him, even those below his rank.

The path of the voyage took the ship south along the coast of France and Portugal, then through the Strait of Gibraltar separating Europe from Africa and into the Mediterranean. As the ship passed through the Suez Canal, Ernest got his first look at barren, sandy desert. After exiting the Red Sea, they crossed the Arabian Sea, steamed around the tip of India, crossed the Indian Ocean, and moved on through the Malacca Strait. After passing Singapore, they headed north to Japan.

After visiting ports in Japan and China, taking on cargo, the *Monmouthshire* sailed to the United States, docking in New York, Newport News, and Fernandina, Florida. In Florida the ship loaded cargo for Hamburg, Antwerp, and London. Being in port was Ernest's busiest time. He had to check all cargo loaded aboard and ensure that it was stowed properly in the hold. The cargo had to be lashed down to keep it from moving while at sea and prevent the ship from listing. While in Florida, Ernest picked up some personal cargo—a brood of baby alligators he intended to take home to Aberdeen House and place in the family's garden pond.

Seven months after embarking on the *Monmouthshire* from London, Ernest and his fast-growing alligators were back in Sydenham. Ernest's family were glad to see him, but not the alligators. The creatures terrified his sisters and the maids, and it wasn't long before Ernest's father arranged for the new pets to be relocated to the London Zoo.

After ten days at home Ernest was off again, on the *Monmouthshire*'s repeat run to the Far East. On this voyage he studied for his first mate's examination, which he passed when he returned to England. With his new ranking, Ernest transferred to the *Flintshire*, another Welsh Shire Line steamer, on which he spent the next year sailing around the world.

Then, for the first time in eight years, Ernest was at home for his birthday on February 15, 1897, when he turned twenty-three. He was home again in June that year. During this time Ernest's sister Kathleen brought her friend Emily Dorman to visit Aberdeen House. Ernest was instantly attracted to Emily, a tall brunette with sparkling blue eyes. What he really liked was her love of poetry and art. He had read so much about these topics aboard ships but found few people interested in discussing them. In Emily he found such a person. He hoped that perhaps one day they would have a future together. Emily soon let Ernest know that she shared no such hope. She was twenty-nine years old, six years older than Ernest, and was not interested in becoming a sailor's wife. Ernest was undaunted by Emily's offhandedness. He found her fascinating and made her promise to write to him at sea.

Ernest spent the next several months sailing aboard the *Flintshire* before returning home once more. When he got home, Ernest was relieved to find that Emily was still single, even if she did take little notice of him.

Ernest remained undeterred. He was convinced that Emily was the woman for him, and he visited her at every available opportunity. They discussed poetry and painting, and Emily accompanied him on a visit to the British Museum and the National Gallery. Ernest also met her father, Charles Dorman, a widower and a well-respected senior partner in a London law firm. The two men got along well, especially since Emily's father loved talking about the orchids he grew and Ernest was knowledgeable of his father's hobby of growing roses. However, Mr. Dorman told Ernest he would never allow any of his three daughters to marry a man who couldn't keep her in style. Ernest took this as a challenge. By the time he returned to sea he was determined to find a way to earn more money and marry Emily. At sea Ernest studied hard and in April passed the exam for his master's certificate. At twenty-four years of age, Ernest Shackleton was now qualified to take command of any ship in the British merchant marine service.

By midsummer 1898 Ernest was back in England for a month. He spent much of it at the Dormans' country home in Tidebrook, Sussex. At the end of July, the *Flintshire* sailed, with Ernest as second officer. He promised to write to Emily from every port he visited and made her promise to write as well.

Ernest hoped to be home for Christmas 1898. Instead he was off the east coast of England battling a winter gale. The next day, Boxing Day, the *Flintshire* ran aground off Redcar in northern England. Knowing it would be several weeks before the ship was repaired and returned to sea, Ernest asked for time off for a visit home.

Rather than heading straight to Sydenham for his father's fifty-second birthday, Ernest visited Emily at her home. She was surprised to see him but invited him in for a cup of tea in the conservatory. Ernest grew nervous once more talking to Emily about his feelings for her. Would she laugh at him again? The conversation became intense. Ernest threw caution to the wind and told Emily he loved her. That seemed to have an effect on her, and she promised to keep an open mind about marrying him.

On New Year's Day 1899, Ernest decided it was time for a new chapter in his life. He needed a job at sea that offered better prospects for a man wanting to marry and have a family. Again he called on his friend Owen Burne, hoping that he would introduce him to the right contact. With his new master's certificate and the right introduction from Owen, it wasn't hard for Ernest to land a position with the Union Castle Line.

Ernest was assigned to the steamer *Tantallon Castle*, one of two vessels authorized to carry the Royal

Mail between London and Cape Town, South Africa. This meant that the ship followed a regular schedule and Ernest would be back in England every three months, with a month off before sailing again. Even though he was only fourth mate on the vessel, Ernest viewed it as a promotion because of the regular schedule. The *Tantallon Castle* also carried passengers, whom Ernest looked forward to getting to know.

Ernest always enjoyed his time back in England between sailings of the *Tantallon Castle.* He especially liked the time he got to spend with Emily.

When at sea, one topic that often came up in Ernest's conversations with passengers was the situation in South Africa. Tensions between the Dutch farmers, known as Boers, and the English settlers there were reaching the breaking point. There had been an uneasy peace between them since the early 1880s, when the Boers and the British fought over who would control the Transvaal and the Orange Free State. The Boers proved to be skilled fighters, and in the end the British government signed a peace treaty giving the Boers self-government in Transvaal and the Orange Free State under minimal British oversight. Soon afterward gold was discovered in Transvaal, and the British forced the Boers to allow thousands of prospectors from the British Empire onto their land. These new immigrants soon outnumbered the Boers and began asking for the right to vote. This was too much for the Boers, who felt that their way of life and identity were being threatened. Now the two sides were trying to reach a compromise.

In June 1899 negotiations between the British and the Boers broke down. On October 9 the Boer president of the South African Republic gave the British government forty-eight hours to withdraw all troops from their borders. The British did nothing, and two days later the Boer War began.

Following the start of the war Ernest was transferred to the *Tintagel Castle*, whose job it was to carry British troops from Southampton to Cape Town, South Africa. Ernest's younger brother Frank had joined the Royal Irish Fusiliers and was preparing to leave to fight in the Boer War.

The *Tintagel Castle* sailed in early 1900. Ernest was assigned the task of boosting morale among the men, possibly the best job he had ever had aboard a ship. His mind worked overtime thinking up ways to keep the men busy on the voyage to Cape Town. He spent hours teaching the military officers semaphore, the method sailors used to signal each other with flags. He also organized concerts and sporting events, and when they sailed over the equator, he staged an impressive ceremony welcoming Father Neptune for the first crossing of the line for the men.

Ernest made many friends among the members of the British army on the ship. One was Cedric Longstaff, a lieutenant with the Surrey Regiment. Ernest recognized his surname right away; Cedric was the son of Llewellyn Longstaff, part owner of a business that produced oil paint in Hull. The business had made Llewellyn Longstaff very wealthy, and recently he had donated twenty-five thousand pounds through the Royal Geographical Society to help fund a British expedition to explore Antarctica. Having joined the Royal Geographical Society the year before to stay informed of the latest explorations going on around the world, Ernest had read about the proposed expedition. It was being called the National Antarctic Expedition, and the British government had promised forty thousand pounds in matching funds to the endeavor. The expedition's goal was to conduct a scientific exploration of the Ross Ice Shelf with the hope of one day using the area as a staging point for an attempt to reach the South Pole. A new ship was currently being built for the expedition, but as yet no crew members had been assigned to her.

Immediately Ernest saw his opportunity. He asked Cedric for a letter of introduction to his father, figuring he might be able to use Llewellyn Longstaff's influence to secure a place on the expedition. It was an exciting prospect to think about.

Ernest also became good friends with the *Tintagel Castle*'s surgeon, Dr. McLean. The two men realized they were part of a historic event and wanted to document it. They decided to produce a book on the voyage, which they titled *O.H.M.S.: A Record of the Voyage of the* Tintagel Castle, *conveying 1,200 volunteers from Southampton to Cape Town, March 1900.* The manuscript for the book contained many photographs showing all aspects of life aboard a troopship. Many of the soldiers wanted their families to see what their lives were like. Subscriptions of two shillings and sixpence were collected from two thousand men to have the book printed and delivered to family back in England.

When he arrived in Cape Town, Ernest bought several newspapers to catch up on what was happening in the world. What caught his attention was a report on an expedition to Antarctica. This expedition had been carried out by Carsten Borchgrevink, a flamboyant Norwegian Australian with a British mother. In 1894 he had become the first man to set foot on Antarctica. Following this achievement, he raised money in London for his own adventure, which he called the Southern Cross Expedition. The expedition's goal had been to get as close as possible to the South Pole. According to the newspaper report, Borchgrevink had made it as far south as latitude 78 degrees 50 minutes. The race to be first man to reach the South Pole was now on.

Returning to England at the end of May 1900, Ernest took five months' leave so that he and Dr. McLean could get their book printed and distributed. Three months later, in August, the book was finished and a specially bound copy was presented to Queen Victoria.

Ernest had another reason to take some leave. He wanted to pursue joining the National Antarctic Expedition. Soon after he returned to England, an article appeared in the *Times* newspaper reporting that a young naval lieutenant named Robert Falcon Scott had been named commander of the expedition. Ernest's spirits rose as he read that Scott "possesses one absolutely essential qualification for polar work—youth." The article went on to say that Scott's lack of experience on the ice was a "small matter; any competent young officer will soon make himself familiar with what has to be done and what remains to do." Ernest's hopes soared. He felt that he had a real chance at being included on the expedition. If youth and competent seamanship were what they needed, he fit the bill perfectly.

Chapter 6

Holds, Stores, and Provisions

Ernest lost no time arranging a meeting with Llewellyn Longstaff. Since Longstaff had donated a quarter of the three-year National Antarctic Expedition's estimated cost, Ernest thought he might be able to make some connections and get his application to the top of the pile. Arriving for the meeting, Ernest wondered what to say to impress the man. He didn't have to say much. Longstaff mostly wanted to hear about his son's time aboard the *Tintagel Castle* with Ernest on the way to fight in the Boer War. By the time Ernest had finished describing the voyage details, Llewellyn Longstaff was ready to help him any way he could. Ernest left the Wimbledon mansion feeling confident that Longstaff would do what he could to get him on the expedition. The next step was to apply.

On September 13, 1900, Ernest wrote to volunteer for the National Antarctic Expedition. He hoped for a quick reply, but as time dragged on, he joined the Union Castle Line ship *Gaika* as third officer, making a round-trip to Cape Town.

When he discovered on his arrival back in England that no decision had been made on his expedition application, Ernest joined the *Carisbrooke Castle* as third officer. He sailed from Southampton on January 5, 1901. He returned in early March 1901 to find Great Britain in mourning. On January 22, while Ernest was at sea, Queen Victoria had died after sixty-three years on the throne. King Edward VII was now the monarch. Ernest could sense that unsettledness had descended over the country. The queen had ruled over a long, prosperous era, and no one was sure what was ahead. The Boer War was supposed to be over in weeks, yet it still dragged on as the Boers showed a stubbornness the British hadn't anticipated.

After arriving home, Ernest went to collect his mail at the Union Castle Line office. He flipped nervously through the envelopes, one of which bore the logo of the National Antarctic Expedition. He slit it open and read the letter inside. He had been accepted for the expedition and appointed third officer of the *Discovery*, the new ship being built.

Ernest soon made his way to the expedition's offices in the old London University building. Captain Robert Falcon Scott greeted him. The two men sat at a large oak table to talk. Ernest quickly realized that they were both similar in some ways but different in others. Robert was six years older than Ernest, thinner, and much more formal. He had joined the Royal Navy at thirteen as a cadet and had risen steadily through the ranks by meeting the right people and following orders. Yet even though he had been a cadet and an officer longer than Ernest, Robert had taken more shore leave, so both men had accumulated the same number of sailing hours. The biggest difference between the two was that Ernest had spent years on a sailing ship, something Robert had not done. Since the *Discovery* was primarily a sailing ship, Ernest felt he had an advantage.

As they talked, Ernest looked around the office. Sleds were stacked in one corner, and a mass of fur-lined clothes hung in another. Ernest felt a surge of excitement realizing that one day soon he would be wearing some of those clothes. Despite the bustling office around him, Ernest was surprised to learn from Robert just how much still needed to be done.

As third officer, Ernest would be in charge of holds, stores, and provisions. He would also be responsible for entertainment aboard ship. He was expected to collect and stow enough supplies to keep the expedition going for three years. The supplies fell into two groups. There were the stores needed to keep the ship running: coal and all the various foodstuffs to keep the men well fed. And then he needed to secure and stow all the stores and equipment necessary to achieve the expedition's goals. This included materials to build huts in Antarctica and items to outfit the huts: furniture, pots, pans, a stove, eating utensils, and plates.

Ernest also had to organize the equipment for the various sledging expeditions, including tents and rations. The rations were based on pemmican, which Ernest learned consisted of ground dried meat mixed with fat, into which water was added and the mixture heated over a stove, creating something between soup and a stew. If other meat was available, it could be added to the mix to make it more hearty. Hard biscuits fortified with gluten were used to thicken the "hoosh," as cooked pemmican was called. Besides pemmican and biscuits, to round out the sledging rations, Ernest needed cheese, chocolate, cocoa, sugar, oatmeal, pea flour, and "red ration," a ground bacon mixture. In addition, Ernest had to gather scripts, dresses, wigs, and costumes for the men to use for putting on shows, as well as footballs, a library of interesting books, a typewriter—anything that might entertain the men during the expedition.

Ernest threw his energy into the preparations. Telegraph messages flowed between London and New Zealand, the *Discovery*'s last stop before Antarctica, to arrange for the ship to be restocked with fresh meat, fruits, and vegetables. Ernest also had to arrange for more coal to be loaded aboard in both South Africa and New Zealand.

By now the Dorman family had moved to Wetherby Gardens in South Kensington, part of London. Ernest tried to spend as much time with Emily as possible, but to his dismay, he learned that she was interested in another man. The news only made him redouble his efforts to woo her.

One of the first people Ernest met in his new position was Sir Clements Markham. At seventy years of age, Sir Clements had been either the secretary or the president of the Royal Geographical Society for nearly forty years. He knew hundreds of explorers, scientists, and naval men. He was also from Yorkshire, and although the Shackleton family had lived in Ireland for over 150 years, they were originally from Yorkshire. Sir Clements pronounced Ernest a fellow Yorkshire man and invited him to meals with his family and friends.

Sir Clements often liked to talk about his time aboard HMS *Assistance*, which on a later voyage, in 1851, was one of four ships sent to learn what happened to the *Erebus* and the *Terror.* These two ships, carrying 129 men, were on an expedition to explore the Arctic. HMS *Assistance* found nothing. It wasn't until fifteen years later that the world learned that both ships had become icebound and were eventually abandoned by their crews, who set out to trek south overland to safety. The men all died along the way from hypothermia, scurvy, and starvation. Ernest had read about the disaster and was fascinated by what Sir Clements had to tell him. It was a reminder of the dangers they could face exploring Antarctica.

One by one, Ernest met the *Discovery*'s other four officers. At thirty-seven years of age, Albert Armitage, second-in-command, was the oldest officer. He was also the only other officer not recruited from the Royal Navy. Ernest liked his easygoing style and his merchant marine background. He liked Reggie Skelton too. Reggie was both chief engineer and the expedition's photographer. Charles Royds was executive officer. While he seemed a patient man, to Ernest he was a navy man through and through—formal, punctual, and always immaculately dressed in his uniform. He was over six feet tall, the tallest of the officers. Michael Barne, the second officer, was another navy man but much less formal than Charles Royds and Captain Scott. He would keep records of the voyage, conduct deep-sea temperature research, and help Albert Armitage with magnetic studies.

Although the National Antarctic Expedition wasn't an official naval expedition, Robert Scott asked the officers to sign an agreement stating that they would abide by naval rules while aboard ship. The expedition's scientific staff and other crew members signing on were also expected to sign the agreement and voluntarily accept Royal Navy conditions and routines. As Ernest affixed his signature to the agreement, he wondered whether he could actually fit into the naval way of doing things. In the navy the gulf between officers and seamen was strictly maintained. Being an Irishman, Ernest prided himself on getting along with just about anyone, regardless of rank.

Two weeks after joining the expedition, Ernest was sent north to Dundee, Scotland, with Charles Royds to oversee the acceptance sea trials of the newly launched *Discovery*. It was Ernest's first time to see the ship. She was a 172-foot-long, wooden-hulled vessel with three masts, rigged as a barque, and fitted with an auxiliary steam engine. Ernest sailed aboard the *Discovery* as the ship was put through her sea trials. It was then that he noticed the vessel's faults. The masts were too short and badly placed, causing her to carry too much sail aft and not enough forward. Although she had an auxiliary steam engine, the coal bunkers were too small to allow the engine to be used for long periods at sea. And the shallow, flat hull with no protrusions, designed to help the *Discovery* in the ice, caused her to roll badly under sail in the open sea.

The best wooden ships for polar work were built in Norway, where the shipbuilding cost was half the price. But the *Discovery* was Sir Clements Markham's pet project. Sir Clements had had the ship designed to his specifications by a naval ship designer and decided she should be British built. Ernest knew that it would be a bad idea to criticize the *Discovery*. It was too late, and Sir Clements did not like to be wrong. All Ernest could do now was hope they could work out some of the ship's flaws on the way south.

In early June 1901, the *Discovery* arrived in London and tied up at the East India Docks. Ernest went to work stowing in the hold the stores he had gathered. He also set up a library in the wardroom, where books ranging from scientific journals to the classics were arranged on shelves attached to the roof beams.

During this time Ernest learned two new skills. He was sent to a training course with the Royal Engineers to learn how to fly a tethered balloon, since the expedition was taking a hydrogen balloon south to use to get a better view of the Antarctic landscape. Ernest also learned how to detonate explosives in the event the *Discovery* became stuck in the ice and needed to be dynamited free.

As the day of the *Discovery*'s departure approached, the full crew of fifty officers, scientists, and crewmen took up residence aboard. Four days before the ship sailed, Dr. Hugh Mill, the Royal Geographical Society's forty-year-old librarian, was asked to come aboard and sail with the ship. Although he had weak eyesight and a frail body, he had a well-rounded knowledge of science. It would be his job to sort out the muddle of scientific instruments aboard and pull the scientific team together. He would disembark in Madeira and return to England.

Two days before departure, Ernest visited his bedridden mother to say goodbye. He also visited Emily. By now she had stopped seeing the other man and told Ernest she would consider marrying him on his return from the expedition. Ernest breathed a sigh of relief. His determination to woo Emily had paid off.

On July 31, 1901, everything was ready and the *Discovery* was due to sail. Ernest had neatly stowed everything for the expedition in the hold and arranged for the ship to be reprovisioned in Lyttelton, New Zealand. There they would also take aboard twenty-three sledge dogs.

Most of the Shackleton clan were at the East India Docks as Ernest boarded ship. Ernest's three youngest sisters were farther downstream at the Royal Albert Dock. As the *Discovery* sailed by them they flashed their brother a semaphore message. Ernest grinned when he saw it. He had taught them all semaphore. He grabbed his handkerchief and borrowed another one from a crewman and signaled them back.

The crew got to know each other as the *Discovery* sailed through the English Channel headed westward. Before setting out into the Atlantic Ocean, the ship and crew had one more duty to perform. King Edward VII had commanded Captain Scott to bring the *Discovery* to Cowes, on the Isle of Wight on England's south coast. The king was visiting Cowes Week, a regatta attended by hundreds of yachtsmen.

At Cowes, bagpipes wailed as King Edward boarded the *Discovery*. The king wore his full admiral's uniform, and the crew, including Ernest, were all dressed in Royal Navy uniforms. Sir Clements had used his contacts to get Ernest a position in the Royal Navy Reserve.

With pomp and ceremony, the king inspected the ship, asking many questions about her and about the expedition. Before disembarking the *Discovery*, he wished the men going south Godspeed on their journey.

The last thing Ernest did before the *Discovery* sailed from Cowes on August 6, 1901, was to go ashore and mail the letter he had written to Mr. Dorman asking for Emily's hand in marriage.

Chapter 7

The Seventh Continent

For Ernest, life aboard the *Discovery* was comfortable. His quarters were one of the ten private cabins off the wardroom reserved for officers and senior scientists. Eating meals in the officers' mess was like dining at a London club. Meals were served by a steward on Royal Doulton china and eaten with engraved silverware.

Several days after the *Discovery* sailed, Dr. Hugh Mill asked Ernest to take charge of checking the water density of the ocean several times a day. He explained that although there were scientists aboard, somehow many opportunities to gather scientific information had been overlooked. Ernest agreed and soon learned to use a hydrometer.

Ernest had other tasks to fit into his day. The stores needed to be checked to make sure they were in good condition. He also took his turn on watch. This was particularly challenging. Ernest had more sailing experience than the other officers aboard and felt the burden of making sure that the *Discovery* sailed at top speed. Even then, the ship was frustratingly slow, averaging only seven or eight knots. As he had noted on the sea trial off Dundee, the shape of the hull caused her to roll badly, making the progress under sail uncomfortable, no matter how Ernest set the sails.

On August 15 the ship reached the Portuguese island of Madeira. Dr. Mill disembarked to return to England. As he said goodbye to Hugh, Ernest was sure he had made a friend for life.

After Hugh left, Ernest became friends with Edward Wilson, a Cambridge-educated doctor. At twenty-nine years of age, Edward served as the junior surgeon aboard. He shared Ernest's love of poetry and would often join him on watch, where the two passed the hours reciting poems to each other and discussing their meaning.

Several days after leaving Madeira, Ernest discovered a serious problem on a routine check of the stores. The hold was flooded. In some places it was neck-deep in water. Cases of food had been inundated and their contents were rotting, creating an unbearable stench.

Ernest took charge of the situation. He had a ventilation shaft drilled from the hold to the deck above to improve air circulation and help dissipate the foul smell. Then he called together the crew, including scientists and doctors, to help unload the stores onto the deck so they could be cleaned and repacked. The rotting food was dumped overboard. The hold was pumped out and disinfected, and a new, higher floor was built. It took several days before Ernest had everything cleaned, repacked, and again stowed in the hold.

On August 31 the *Discovery* crossed the equator and headed for Trindade Island, an isolated, rocky outcrop in the Atlantic, 750 miles off the coast of Brazil. Captain Scott planned to stop there so that the scientists aboard could collect plants, insects, and geological specimens.

From Trindade Island, the *Discovery* headed for Cape Town, where it would take on more coal. The ship arrived there in early October. Ernest hoped to see his brother while in Cape Town, but he learned that Frank had been wounded in the fighting and shipped back to England. Ernest found Cape Town depressing. The Boer War dragged on, and in the harbor he watched as thousands of captured Boer women and children were loaded onto ships to be sent from South Africa to Ceylon and India as prisoners of war.

The *Discovery* was over a week behind schedule on arrival in Cape Town. Captain Scott decided to skip their planned stop in Melbourne, Australia, and head straight for New Zealand. The decision left Ernest scrambling. Waiting to be loaded onto the *Discovery* in Melbourne were tons of supplies and the sections of three prefabricated wooden huts for use on the ice. Telegraphs flowed between Cape Town and Melbourne. Soon Ernest had arranged for everything in Melbourne to be shipped to Lyttelton, New Zealand, to await the *Discovery's* arrival.

From Cape Town, the *Discovery* headed south into the Roaring Forties, a belt roughly between latitude 40 and 50 degrees south, where westerly winds blow. Since there are few land masses to impede the wind at that latitude, the winds blow steadily at thirty to forty miles per hour. Ernest was surprised at how fast the ship sped along before the steady wind.

The *Discovery* stopped at Macquarie Island, halfway between New Zealand and Antarctica, to gather more specimens.

The *Discovery* dropped anchor outside Lyttelton Harbour on New Zealand's South Island late on Thursday night, November 28, 1901. Eager for news from home, Ernest took one of the ship's boats and rowed ashore at two o'clock in the morning. He woke the postmaster to collect the mail. Back on the *Discovery*, the first letter Ernest opened was from Mr. Dorman. The answer was yes, Ernest could marry Emily. His elation turned to shock with the second letter, in which Emily described how her father had died suddenly. Ernest wished that he could be there to comfort Emily, and he wondered what else might happen in the three years he would be out of contact.

At daylight the *Discovery* steamed into Lyttelton Harbour and moored beside a British naval ship named HMS *Ringarooma*. Once the ship docked, most of the seamen went ashore. The officers remained aboard. Ernest had a lot to do. The hold needed to be emptied so that the leaky hull could be repaired.

The cargo needed to be inspected, repacked, and restowed, along with the prefabricated hut sections sent on from Melbourne and the tons of other stores that had been ordered to replenish the ship.

Having been at sea for nearly seven weeks, the *Discovery*'s crew caused problems ashore. They drank in the pubs and brawled. The situation got so bad that several of the men were laid off. Others jumped ship rather than face discipline. Captain Scott arranged for replacement crewmen from the *Ringarooma.* Among the sailors who transferred to the *Discovery* was a twenty-four-year-old Irishman named Tom Crean. Tom was three years younger than Ernest, but the two Irishmen understood and appreciated each other immediately.

It was summer in the Southern Hemisphere, and with the approach of Christmas, the weather was warm, but Ernest hardly had time to enjoy it. He worked hard stowing provisions, including forty-five live sheep to be used for fresh meat and twenty-three sled dogs shipped to New Zealand to go on the expedition. The sheep bleated and the dogs barked loudly until at last everything was stowed aboard. Ernest knew the *Discovery* was overloaded, but the expedition would be gone for three years, and it seemed that little could be left behind.

Louis Bernacchi, an Italian-born Australian physicist and astronomer, joined the ship in Lyttelton. Everyone seemed glad to have him aboard, since he was the only crew member with firsthand experience in Antarctica. He had wintered at Cape Adare three years before as part of Carsten Borchgrevink's

Southern Cross Expedition. Louis settled into the cabin next to Ernest's.

On December 21, 1901, the *Discovery* set sail down the coast of the South Island to its next stop, Port Chalmers, where an extra forty-five tons of coal were loaded aboard. Since the hold was already full, the coal was stowed on deck.

On Christmas Eve, the *Discovery* sailed south from New Zealand. Nine days later Charles Royds spotted the first chunk of floating pack ice. He called everyone to see it. Ernest watched how it hung low in the water, the waves sometimes rolling across it. He knew they would encounter much more ice like this very soon.

Several hours later, the *Discovery* crossed the Antarctic Circle. Louis explained to Ernest that this was the northernmost latitude in the Southern Hemisphere where the sun can remain continuously above or below the horizon for twenty-four hours. Every location south of the Antarctic Circle experiences at least one day each year when the sun doesn't set, and another day when it doesn't rise.

The plan was for the *Discovery* to scout the coast of Antarctica, going in an easterly direction, until they found a sheltered bay in which the ship could winter over. More and more pack ice lay in front of the ship as it steamed south toward the Ross Sea. The crew at last caught the first glimpse on the horizon of something that few others had ever seen: the seventh continent, nearly the size of South America. Ernest could make out the Admiralty Range of Victoria Land bathed in golden light from the midnight sun. He knew that he would never forget his first sighting of Antarctica.

On January 9, 1902, the *Discovery* anchored off Cape Adare. A boat was lowered over the side, and Ernest was one of the men in it. He was about to set foot on the frozen continent for the first time. On reaching shore, the men pulled the boat onto the shingle beach and were immediately surrounded by thousands of Adélie penguins squawking loudly. The stench of penguin excrement filled the air. Ernest made his way over to the hut built by Carsten Borchgrevink and his men, including Louis Bernacchi, in which they had wintered. It was the only man-made structure on the entire continent. At the hut they left a note explaining who they were and where the *Discovery* was bound so that if they did not return, a search party would know they had made it that far.

Back on the *Discovery* the men headed down the coast, following the course of Captain James Ross, who sixty years before had named the area Victoria Land in honor of the queen. Ross had led an expedition of two ships, the *Erebus* and the *Terror,* to locate the South Magnetic Pole. They were the same two ships that later were lost on John Franklin's Arctic expedition.

On the horizon, smoke from Mount Erebus, a volcano, formed a plume in the sky above Ross Island. Mount Terror, a second volcanic cone, rose next to it. On January 22 the *Discovery* rounded Cape Crozier, the most easterly point of Ross Island. Before them lay the Ross Ice Shelf, a sheet of ice whose sheer cliffs rose 160 feet into the air in places. Impressive as that was, Ernest knew that far more ice was lurking beneath them.

With the weather holding, Captain Scott announced that they would sail along the face of the ice shelf toward King Edward VII Land. After eight days of sailing and charting, he decided it was time to come about and find a good spot to winter. On February 3, 1902, the *Discovery* anchored off a part of the Ross Ice Shelf that sloped gently to the water's edge. Captain Scott, Ernest, and Reggie Skelton went ashore to explore. They strapped skis to their feet, but none of them had ever used them before. Skis proved harder to manage than Ernest had imagined. The three men slid and pulled themselves only a short distance before giving up and returning to the ship.

Captain Scott then decided to survey the land from the air. The balloon was brought out of the hold and transferred to the ice, along with the hydrogen cylinders to fill it. Ernest expected to be the first aloft, since he had received special training in how to handle the balloon. However, Captain Scott announced that he would go first, telling Ernest that he wanted "the honour of being the first aeronaut to make an ascent in the Antarctic regions." Ernest went up in the balloon next, climbing to 650 feet, higher than the captain. He was tethered to the ground by a wire cable. While aloft he took the first aerial photographs of Antarctica.

The plan was to send two more men up in the balloon, but the balloon had a faulty valve, and all the hydrogen had leaked out of it during launch. It was now useless. The men named the location

Balloon Bight. The *Discovery* loaded up the men and headed toward Mount Erebus in the distance. On February 8 they reached McMurdo Sound, a waterway bounded on one side by South Victoria Land and on the other by Ross Island. Later that day the *Discovery* dropped anchor off a spot near the southern limit of Ross Island, which they christened Winter Quarters Bay.

The men still had two months before Antarctica would be plunged into darkness for four months, and Captain Scott wanted to make the most of the time. The prefabricated huts were off-loaded, and the men began erecting them on a rocky peninsula ashore, which they called Hut Point. After the huts were erected, Captain Scott announced that expedition members would continue living and working aboard ship, with the huts being used for storage and shelter. The sled dogs were off-loaded from the ship, and it was soon discovered that no one aboard knew how to get them to pull a sledge. Several men tried, but the dogs were aggressive. In fact, several dogs died in vicious fights with each other.

Once everything was settled and the *Discovery* was secured and ready for winter, Captain Scott announced that there was time for a short expedition inland to scout out the land. This would pave the way for longer travels when the sun came up again in August. It was a wonderful twenty-eighth birthday present for Ernest when he was chosen to lead the team south.

On Wednesday, February 19, 1902, Ernest dressed himself in preparation for his foray on the ice. He pulled on two pairs of thick woolen socks and then pulled Burberry trousers over his woolen long pants and then put on a Burberry shirt. These two items were made of gabardine, a cotton fabric that was light, wind and water resistant, and hard wearing. He fastened a belt around his middle. Over the socks he put on *finnesko*, reindeer-skin boots. With leather thongs he tied on crampons to the bottom of each boot. Last, he pulled on his Burberry helmet, which had a knitted balaclava inside and was covered by the same gabardine fabric as the trousers and shirt. With the helmet on, all that was visible of Ernest's face was his eyes, nose, and mouth. Around his neck hung a pair of wolf-skin fur gloves attached to a cord.

Ernest joined his friend Dr. Edward Wilson and Hartley Ferrar, the twenty-three-year-old Cambridge graduate who was the expedition's geologist. The three men set out on their trek, pulling, or man-hauling as they called it, their sledge and a pram, a small Norwegian-designed boat for use in case the ice gave way beneath them. Fourteen days' worth of food rations, weighed out and placed in a separate bag for each day, along with their tent, furs, Primus stove, fuel, and cooking utensils were loaded onto the sledge. The crew of the *Discovery* cheered as the trio set off. Each man had made a personal pennant to fly on the back of the sledge. Ernest's contained the Shackleton family crest and the family motto "By endurance we conquer."

This was the expedition's first journey inland, and Ernest chose their goal: White Island, a bare, rocky outcrop protruding through the ice to the south. Looking across the sea of white, Ernest estimated that it was ten miles away. The ice was hard and compact, which made the going easy for the first two or three miles. Then the wind, which had been light when they set out, began to whip around them, until they were in a blizzard. Ernest was surprised. Because he had read that Antarctica was a desert where it hardly ever snowed inland, he wondered where all the snow was coming from. Edward explained that the snowflakes were actually ice particles that were whipped up from the ground and flung around by the wind. The going became tough, so tough that the men shuffled forward six inches at a time. They kept moving. Ernest was sure that they could make it to the rocky outcrop before they camped.

After battling through the blizzard for twelve hours, the men were exhausted. Ernest gave the order to make camp. This led to another problem—none of them had ever pitched this kind of tent before, and now they had to do it in a blizzard. By now Ernest's ears had surface frostbite, and one of his hands was white and numb. Yet somehow, hanging on to the tent poles so they wouldn't fly away in the wind, they managed to erect the tent. They crawled inside and prepared to cook some hoosh. Here they encountered the next hurdle—lighting the Primus stove, another first for the men. With much trial and error under extreme conditions, they discovered how to light it and were able to prepare their hoosh.

Ernest had read many stories that involved men sleeping in tents, but he had never done so himself. He took off his boots, wriggled into his sleeping suit, and settled down to sleep on the furs laid over the tent floor. As he lay there, the wind howled outside. Ernest wondered whether Sir Clements and Robert Scott really had the right idea. Had it been wise to take a group of young, inexperienced men to the most inhospitable place on earth and expect them to figure out how to survive? It might have been wiser to choose men with experience or, dare he think it, to investigate how others, such as the Norwegians or the Russians, carried out their polar exploration. Yes, they had brought along sled dogs, which the Norwegians used to tow their sledges through snow and ice, but they had brought no one with them who knew how to properly handle the dogs and get them to pull the sledges. This was because Captain Scott believed that man-hauling their sledges across the ice was far more noble than letting dogs do the work.

Of course, it was too late now to consider why the expedition hadn't been better prepared. Ernest was in a tent on the ice in a blizzard. His goal was getting the three of them to White Island and back safely to the ship.

Chapter 8

Into the White Wilderness

Two hours after drifting off to sleep, Ernest awoke to an eerie silence. The wind had died down. This was an opportunity they couldn't miss. He woke the other two men, and the trio quickly packed up their camp, throwing everything onto the sledge. They made good time, and after several hours' man-hauling the sledge, they were within a mile of White Island. Now the ice between them and the island had broken into large, uneven chunks. Because there was no way to pull a sledge over it, Ernest had them make camp once more. They slept for eight hours. Afterward they left the tent and most of their supplies and began clambering over the rough ice.

When they reached the island, they climbed to the top of a rocky promontory, from which Ernest could see the vastness of the ice shelf and an unknown mountain range in the distance. Using a theodolite, he took a reading on the sun and worked out their position. The men watched the sun set. It was a glorious moment for Ernest, sitting atop an island no man had ever set foot on.

Even though the sun had set, in the lingering twilight the men climbed down and made their way back to their tent and supplies. The following morning, they set out at a fast pace for the *Discovery*. The weather held, and they reached the ship in eleven hours. When they arrived, Ernest did some calculations and discovered they had walked forty miles, not the ten or twenty he had supposed. When he met with the other officers for a debriefing, Ernest explained how unprepared they had been and how lucky they were to have all made it back in one piece. He suggested a number of issues that should be addressed before any more men headed out into the white wilderness around them.

Two weeks later another group set out. This time a group of twelve men were led by Charles Royds. In the polar twilight they were headed for Cape Crozier, a prearranged rendezvous, where they would leave a message for any relief ship that might be looking for them. After his experience, Ernest wasn't sure that that was a good idea. He discovered that he was right when seven of the men returned to the *Discovery* led by the able seaman Frank Wild.

Frank described how the weather was worse than expected. The men had made slow progress over the ice and risked running out of rations. Charles had decided to send nine men back to the ship under the leadership of Michael Barne, who had never before led men on the ice. On the way back Michael led the men too close to the edge of the ice shelf. One seaman, George Vince, who was wearing flat-soled fur boots, slipped on the ice and plunged down a steep slope toward the sea. The men had no way to rescue him. Afterward Michael fell apart, and Frank stepped forward and led the rest of the men safely back to the ship. Along the way, another member of the party, eighteen-year-old Charles Hare, had wandered off and become lost.

Although the men had little hope that George was still alive, Ernest volunteered to take one of the boats and search for him. Several other men joined him as they made their way among the unfrozen channels of water, or leads, as they were called, amidst the ice. After six hours they gave up, finding no trace of their shipmate.

The next day Charles Royds and the other two men made it back to the ship. They were exhausted, incoherent, and frostbitten, but alive. There was still no sign of Charles Hare. Then, amazingly, the following day, Charles staggered back to the ship. He was surprised that everyone was worried about him. He had lost all sense of time and thought that only a few hours had passed, not two days. He told how he had slept under the snow for a while and then gotten up and headed for the ship. Ernest was astounded that Charles had made it back alive. As he thought back over the whole ordeal, Ernest was most impressed with Frank Wild, who seemed to be a natural leader who knew how to survive in extreme conditions.

No more long excursions were made from the ship in the twilight. On April 23, 1902, winter darkness descended over McMurdo Sound. It would be 120 days before the sun came up again. A large canvas awning was draped over the ship to help keep the warmth in. When the *Discovery* first arrived in Antarctica, electric lights were used on the ship. A windmill placed high on a mast turned the generator that powered the lights, but high winds had damaged its blades, and oil lamps and candles were brought up from the hold to light the ship.

Ernest found plenty to do aboard: plays to stage, using the scripts and costumes he had brought from England; debates to organize among the men; and a newspaper, the *South Polar Times*, to publish. He also had his water density tests to carry out. In addition, he volunteered to work with Edward Wilson to take weather readings each day at Crater Hill on Ross Island. This meant leaving the ship, crossing the ice, and climbing the hill in darkness. Even though the spot wasn't too far from the ship, sometimes it took all Ernest's strength to make it there and back. Still, he enjoyed the experience, especially on clear nights when he could see the Southern Cross shining above and aurora australis, the southern lights, bright and green in the sky. Also, the eerie red volcanic glow from Mount Erebus was clearly visible from Crater Hill.

In mid-June Robert Scott made the announcement the men were waiting for. When the sun came up in August, an expedition from the ship would head south. It was too far to go all the way to the

South Pole, but the expedition would try to reach 85 degrees latitude, about 350 miles from the South Pole. That would be the farthest south any human had been in Antarctica.

Ernest hoped to be chosen for the expedition, but to his surprise Captain Scott decided that only he and Edward would go. That made no sense to Ernest. It seemed unsafe for just two men to walk out onto the ice. If one of them was injured, the other man would have to choose between staying with the injured man and returning to get help. Ernest confided his fears to Edward, and Robert relented, appointing a third man to the team—Ernest Shackleton. Ernest was ecstatic. This was the kind of real adventure he had come south for.

Much had to be done to get the expedition ready. Ernest was put in charge of training the dogs to run in traces pulling the sledges. This was a challenging job, since no one on the ship knew how to go about it. Ernest thought back with regret to the Scottish dog handler whose application Captain Scott had rejected.

Rations also had to be prepared. This involved weighing out pounds and ounces of tea, sugar, cocoa, butter, biscuits, and pemmican and stowing each day's rations in separate numbered and labeled canvas bags. In all, Ernest prepared rations for ninety days, the proposed length of the expedition. Some of the rations would be laid up in depots along the way so that the three men could access them on the return journey, thus limiting the weight they had to haul on the sledges.

As the polar sun rose once more and preparations for the trip were in their final stages, scurvy broke out on the *Discovery.* Spots appeared on the men's skin, the men's gums turned spongy and bled, and they felt fatigued. Everyone had expected the disease sooner or later. No one was sure what caused scurvy. Robert and Edward thought that it was the result of eating unsterilized food or aging canned food. Ernest, on the other hand, believed it was caused by a lack of fresh food. By now the sheep from New Zealand had been killed and eaten, and the men's diet was mainly tinned meat and biscuits. This frustrated Ernest, who had tried to convince Captain Scott to allow them to kill and eat the seals wintering around the ship. The captain had refused. As far as he was concerned, the provisions aboard were good enough. But when scurvy broke out, Ernest was able to lead a team of men seal hunting. Afterward the men began eating seal meat every day, and the scurvy symptoms lessened.

On Sunday, November 2, 1902, with the scurvy taken care of for the time being, Ernest, Robert, and Edward set out on their expedition. They were accompanied by two support parties who would go partway and leave a depot of supplies before returning to the *Discovery.*

At first it seemed that Ernest had trained the dogs enough after all. The animals were put into their traces and harnessed to the sledges, and they pulled well together. A week into the trip, everyone was cold and tired. Captain Scott decided they should have a rest day, as it was Sunday. Edward read to the men from the Bible. The captain read to them from Charles Darwin's *On the Origin of Species*.

The next day the men trudged on. It was minus eleven degrees Fahrenheit, and they were covering about ten miles a day. The last support team trailed behind for another week, until November 15, when they set up a supply depot and transferred more provisions to the three men's sledge. Now each dog had to pull 150 pounds of weight, which they were not so eager to do. After making camp that night, Ernest took a theodolite reading to get their position. They had covered only two and a half miles the whole day. Something had to be done to speed up their advance. They decided the load should be divided in half. One half would be pulled a mile or so on the sledge and the supplies left in the snow. The men and dogs would then return with the sledge for the other half of the supplies. This meant that for every mile they gained, they actually traveled three miles. But since the load would be lighter, they felt they could move faster. This worked for a few weeks, until the dogs refused to pull the sledge on their own. Ernest and Edward harnessed themselves to the traces and pulled alongside the dogs. By now Ernest was weak and hungry. His muscles ached, and it was hard for him to breathe.

On December 9 the first dog collapsed and died, quickly followed by four others. A week later Robert Scott ordered the men to dump most of their supplies at a second depot, which they marked with a black flag. With fewer supplies, they could make better progress. Since the time the last support party had turned back, the men had traveled only 109 miles and still had a long way to go to beat Carsten Borchgrevink's farthest south mark of latitude 78 degrees 50 minutes.

Robert hadn't rationed the men's food properly from the beginning, and the stores were running low. What bothered Ernest was the fact that the men seemed to be in this situation because of Captain Scott's lack of forethought. Every night Ernest dreamed about food. His most recurring dream was of slices of pie flying past him that he was unable to catch no matter how hard he tried.

By now the dog food was gone, and it was decided that the dogs and men would continue pulling the sledge together, and when necessary, one dog would be killed to feed the other dogs. This seemed brutal, but Ernest knew that there was no way that the dogs could get back to the ship with no food.

The team continued trekking south until Edward and Ernest, certain that their lives would soon be in danger, urged Robert to turn around and head back to their supply depot. The captain refused. He wanted to cross the latitude 82 degrees south mark, and it seemed to Ernest that nothing would stop him, not even if it meant losing their lives. Edward and Ernest did manage to get Robert to promise to turn back once they had made it that far.

On December 21, Ernest and Robert again began to show the telltale signs of scurvy. Still the captain refused to turn around. A week later the men crossed latitude 82 degrees 10 minutes south. It was time to turn around and head back, or so Ernest thought. But Captain Scott reneged. This time he said he wanted to inspect some ridges several miles farther south. The weary men slogged on through another storm for four hours before camping. The sun came out, and Ernest used his theodolite to take another reading and chart their position. They were at latitude 82 degrees 15 minutes south. They had beaten Carsten Borchgrevink's farthest south mark by 230 miles.

On January 1, 1903, Robert agreed to turn around and head back. The three men had walked nearly three hundred miles in two months. They had packed enough food supplies for ninety days but had already used more than sixty days' worth. Ernest and Edward talked privately. They both doubted they could make it back. Their only chance was dependent on the weather holding the entire way. Also, their survival depended on their reaching the food depot by January 17, but with a stiff headwind and dropping temperatures, they were doing well to cover one mile an hour. The number of dogs had dwindled, and those alive were hardly any help, even with the men harnessed to the sledge alongside them.

By January 10 the men had thirty-three miles to go to reach the spot where they had offloaded some of their food supplies. Only two dogs were alive, and Ernest had nagging doubts that they would even find the depot. The only thing to guide them to it was the black flag. What if a snowdrift covered it all or a gale had ripped the flag out of the ice? Yet the depot was their only hope. The scurvy had flared up again, and their muscles ached, their gums bled, and their stamina was sapped.

But luck, or providence, as Ernest preferred to call it, was with the men. They covered ten miles a day, reaching the depot on January 13. Ernest should have felt relieved that they now had extra food, but by now he was seriously ill. In addition to his suffering from scurvy, hunger, and exhaustion, his lungs burned when he breathed, and he was coughing up blood. After they set out from the depot, he was forbidden to pull the sledge. Instead he skied or walked alongside it. Once he even had to climb onto the sledge and let the other two men pull him along.

On January 25, 1903, Mount Erebus came into view on the horizon. The men were close to the supply depot that had been set up by the support team before their return to the *Discovery*. In a fit of elation, they ate the last of their food, only to watch a blizzard spring up from the south. Now, unless they found the supply depot within a few hours, they might well die. Despite his illness, Ernest willed himself to ski on as they battled forward. The blizzard bore down on them with a curtain of wind-borne ice particles. In the brief few minutes when the wind died down, Ernest spotted the supply depot. They were saved!

Within hours the three men were eating a hearty meal of hoosh. They camped for the night, but the next morning Ernest could not move. He vaguely heard Edward tell Captain Scott that he would not last much longer. Ernest knew he had to do something. With superhuman effort he crawled to the tent door and lay outside while the men broke camp. They carried him onto the sledge, and off they went again over the ice. At lunchtime, Ernest willed himself up onto his skis to lessen the load of the other two men.

By February 3 the men were counting down the miles to the ship: nine, eight, seven, six. Then Ernest saw two figures coming toward them across the ice. Louis Bernacchi and Reggie Skelton had been sent out to search for them. They took over hauling the sledge the rest of the way back to the ship.

As they approached the *Discovery*, Ernest barely noticed the flags flying or the newly arrived ship, the *Morning*, moored out in the open water nearby. The men on the *Discovery* cheered and waved as the explorers approached. All Ernest wanted was a long, hot bath and a warm bed.

Chapter 9

You Can't Tie an Eagle in a Barnyard

After taking his first bath in ninety-three days, Ernest went to the wardroom for a dinner to celebrate their farthest south trip. He didn't make it through the soup course, however. He was too tired to eat another bite. He excused himself and went to his cabin. Before crawling into his bunk, he reread the letters from Emily that had arrived on the *Morning* while he was away on the trek. He was happy that she still intended to marry him and that her father had left a trust fund that gave her seven hundred pounds a year. Ernest felt that Emily's trust and the money he was earning on the expedition would be enough for the two of them to live modestly while he pursued his goal of finding a job that paid well.

As he drifted off to sleep, Ernest thought about marrying Emily when he returned to England. He didn't know that that was going to be a lot sooner than he thought. A month later, on Monday, March 2, 1903, Ernest was standing on the deck of the *Morning* along with seven other seamen from the *Discovery.* Most of them had asked to be relieved of their duties to return home, but not Ernest. He had been ordered home by Captain Scott because of health problems. He felt humiliated. It was true that he had struggled to rebuild his health following the trek south and that he still coughed a lot, but he didn't think it was enough to justify sending him home. Would people see him as a failure when he got home?

The trip to England took three months, during which Ernest regained his strength. He disembarked ship in London, tanned and fit. His father, sisters, and Emily were there to greet him. Far from being labeled a failure, Ernest was in high demand as the first person able to give a firsthand report on the *Discovery* expedition. Newspapers and magazines clambered for interviews, the Royal Geographical Society consulted him, and a round of parties was held for him to attend.

After some time all the activity died down, and Ernest was faced with what to do next. Emily's older brother, Herbert, who acted as her guardian, wanted him to find a job before they married. Ernest looked around for something that would keep his body and mind busy. He tried for a permanent position in the Royal Navy, but that didn't work out. He turned his attention to public speaking. Ernest had a knack for telling a good story, which he attributed to his

Irish heritage. Soon he discovered he could hold large audiences spellbound with his tales from the extreme south. This led to a position as subeditor of the monthly *Royal Magazine*. Parts of the job suited Ernest. He had enjoyed writing and editing for the *South Polar Times* aboard the *Discovery*, but since the job also required a lot of repetitive paperwork, he soon tired of it.

Next Ernest applied to become secretary of the Royal Scottish Geographical Society in Edinburgh. The society had been formed twenty years before by prominent mapmaker Agnes Bruce, a daughter of the explorer David Livingstone. The post as secretary involved a lot of public speaking as well as arranging talks by interesting people from all over the world. With help from Hugh Mill, Ernest got the job. He moved to Edinburgh in January 1904. He now had a steady income that would satisfy Emily's brother. And now that Ernest had a good job, he and Emily set April 9, 1904, as their wedding date. Ernest took the train down to London for the wedding, and the two were married at Christ Church, Westminster. After the ceremony, the new Mr. and Mrs. Shackleton returned to Edinburgh.

While in London for his wedding, Ernest learned that the *Discovery* had left Antarctica and steamed into Lyttelton Harbour, the first stop on her trip back to England. Things had not gone as planned on the expedition. It had been a cold summer in Antarctica, and the ice encasing the *Discovery* hadn't melted. The British government sent two vessels, the *Morning* and the *Terra Nova*, to McMurdo Sound to rescue her. There were fears that the *Discovery* might have to be abandoned. At the last moment, the crew were able to free their ship by blasting her out of the ice.

On September 18, 1904, eighteen months after leaving Antarctica, Ernest took the train back to London to visit the *Discovery*. The ship was at the East India Docks in London, and Ernest went aboard to attend a welcome-home luncheon. He eagerly shook hands with his old crewmates and reminisced about their time together on the ice. He greeted Robert Scott warmly, and as they ate together, the two seemed to overlook the tension that had developed between them.

Being back on the *Discovery* brought a rush of memories to Ernest and made him feel unsettled. Just as with the subediting job at *Royal Magazine*, being secretary of the Royal Scottish Geographical Society involved a lot of behind-the-scenes work. Ernest found more of his time was taken up with paperwork than with public speaking.

Soon after getting back to Edinburgh, Ernest was approached by the Liberal Unionist Party to be their candidate in the next parliamentary election, in January 1906. This sounded like an interesting challenge to Ernest, especially since it fed his love of public speaking. He accepted the candidacy. Because the election was over a year away, Ernest continued with the Royal Scottish Geographical Society, at least until he needed to put his full-time effort into campaigning.

Emily wasn't enthusiastic about the idea. She was expecting a baby in February and did not relish the upheaval that campaigning would bring to the family. Raymond Swinford Shackleton, a strong, healthy boy was born February 2, 1905, just as Ernest was gearing up for his campaign. In July 1905, he resigned his post with the Royal Scottish Geographical Society and devoted his time to the election, giving speeches, participating in debates, and meeting voters.

Despite his best effort, Ernest lost the election. However, in the course of campaigning, he had made friends with a rich industrialist named William Beardmore. William owned large shipbuilding and steelmaking companies in Glasgow that employed forty thousand men. After the election, he offered Ernest a job. Ernest accepted, commuting fifty miles by train each day from Edinburgh to Glasgow.

It didn't take Ernest long to become restless again. His thoughts turned to Antarctica. As he sat on the train day after day, an idea formed in his mind. Could he get enough private donors, such as William Beardmore, to sponsor him on his own expedition to reach the South Pole? This was something he dared not discuss with Emily, who was pregnant with their second child. Ernest didn't want to burden her unless such an expedition was a real possibility. As he continued pondering the notion, he estimated that such an expedition, including a ship, personnel, and supplies, would cost about seventeen thousand pounds. He decided to set out to see if he could raise the money.

Cecily Jane Shackleton was born two days before Christmas 1906, and early in the new year, Ernest told Emily of his plan to go to Antarctica for two years. She accepted the news, telling Ernest you can't tie an eagle in a barnyard. She recognized that Ernest had tried his hand at many jobs, but clearly his true vocation was being an explorer.

The money for the expedition came in slowly from a variety of sources. Elizabeth Dawson-Lambton, who donated the balloon for the *Discovery,* wrote a check for one thousand pounds. William Beardmore was cautious, offering Ernest a seven-thousand-pound loan against any profits from the expedition.

On February 11, 1907, Ernest went to a meeting at the Royal Geographical Society in London to announce his new expedition to the South Pole. He was in good company. That night, two Norwegian polar explorers, Fridtjof Nansen and Roald Amundsen, were the top-billed speakers. They were followed by Henryk Arctowski, a Polish scientist, who talked about the Belgian plan to use motorized sledges to reach the South Pole. He also reported that the French were building a polar ship to take south. Never before had there been so much interest in reaching the South Pole.

By the end of the evening, Ernest was convinced that someone would reach the South Pole in the next two or three years, and he desperately wanted to win that race, carrying the flag of the British Empire.

Confident others would see it his way, Ernest spent the next day talking to John Scott Keltie, secretary of the Royal Geographical Society, and the society's new president, Sir George Goldie. To Ernest's surprise, neither man would commit to helping him financially or in any other way. In fact, they told him he could not use the Royal Geographical Society's name in any of his brochures or press releases.

Ernest was confused. Like him, the society's secretary and president had heard the same speakers tell stories of the various preparations under way to be the first to reach the South Pole and plant their county's flag there. Why wouldn't the Royal Geographical Society want to back a British expedition to be the first to the South Pole? There seemed no explanation for their actions.

Undeterred, on the train back to Edinburgh Ernest made a list of men he wanted on his expedition, which he had named the British Antarctic Expedition. First on the list was Edward Wilson, whom he thought of as his best friend. Also on the list were others from the *Discovery*: Albert Armitage, Thomas Hodgson, and Reggie Skelton. As soon as he got home, he began contacting these men, offering them a place on the expedition and the chance to bring honor to their country.

One by one, each man turned him down with what Ernest could only conclude were lame excuses. What was going on? He stumbled upon the answer when he asked George Mulock, a young naval lieutenant and an excellent mapper, to join the expedition. Like the others, George turned Ernest down, telling him he had already signed on with Robert Scott's expedition! It was as if a jolt of electricity had shocked Ernest. Suddenly it all made sense: the Royal Geographical Society's refusal to help him or even let him use their name, the weak excuses of every single man he had asked thus far.

Just as Ernest was deciding what to do next, he received a blunt letter from Robert Scott saying that it was his right to go south again and attempt to be the first man to reach the South Pole, and that Ernest had no right to set up an opposing expedition. There was room for only one expedition representing the British Empire, and that was Robert Scott's. Robert also said, "I think anyone who has had anything to do with exploration will regard it [McMurdo Sound] as mine. . . . It must be clear to you now that you have placed yourself in the way of my life's work. If you go to McMurdo Sound you go to winter quarters that are clearly mine." It got worse. Robert accused Ernest of disloyalty for not asking him if he was planning another trip south before announcing his own intentions.

Ernest was frustrated to be stuck in Edinburgh while Robert Scott had free range in London stirring up questions about Ernest's character. Word got back that Robert wanted Ernest to stop all his expedition plans immediately and that if he did not, Ernest was in danger of "ruining the cause of true exploration."

Raising funds was difficult enough, but now, with Robert Scott as a new enemy, it was nearly impossible. Ernest did not sleep for four nights, wondering what he should do. In the end, he visited Edward Wilson for advice. Edward came down squarely on Robert Scott's side. Scott, he argued, had the right to be the next man to use McMurdo Sound. If Ernest could raise the money and gather the men, he should land somewhere else and make his own way inland from there.

Edward's opinion shocked Ernest. He had felt sure that he could count on his friend to be sympathetic. He felt betrayed. Both of them had been to Antarctica, and both knew that using McMurdo Sound gave any expedition a huge advantage in reaching the South Pole. Ross Island was the southernmost piece of land in Antarctica accessible by ship. It was the obvious gateway to the South Pole.

Ernest sought the opinion of other people regarding Robert's claim to McMurdo Sound. Hugh Mill wrote from London assuring Ernest that he completely supported him. "All territories are absolutely open and free to anyone who has the courage, perseverance and good luck to reach it," he wrote.

Still, Ernest agonized over what to do. In the end he decided he would rather lose the chance at making a record than do anything that was not quite right. He met with Robert in London and agreed not to use McMurdo Sound. Instead, he would winter over at King Edward VII Land on the other side of the Ross Ice Shelf or at the Barrier Inlet along the edge of the ice shelf, and he would not venture west of the 170-degree meridian. The arrangement made the British Antarctic Expedition much more dangerous. Now they would have to navigate uncharted waters, but Ernest was glad to have the whole debacle behind him and get back to fundraising and planning.

Ernest needed a ship for the expedition. A two-year-old, six-hundred-ton polar exploration vessel, the *Bjorn*, was up for sale. The ship had good engines, a large hold, and accommodations for fifty men. She was perfect for the expedition. Regrettably, her owners wanted eleven thousand pounds for her, far more than Ernest's expedition budget allowed. Ernest turned to a cheaper alternative, an Arctic sealer named *Nimrod,* built in Dundee, Scotland, in 1866. She was for sale for five thousand pounds, which fit the budget.

Ernest wasn't expecting a perfect vessel, but when he went to inspect the ship, his optimism almost failed him. The fetid stench of old seal oil penetrated every corner of the *Nimrod.* She was forty years old and well worn. Her engine was ready for a major overhaul, and her top speed was little more than six knots. Her masts were in need of repair, she needed new sails, and her holds were filthy. To make matters worse, the *Nimrod* was only 136 feet long. Even to Ernest she looked small, especially since she would be sailing across the roughest stretch of ocean on earth. Yet the vessel fit his budget, and Ernest purchased her.

The *Nimrod* was brought to London and taken to a shipyard for repairs and alterations for the expedition. The old engine was replaced with a new one. New masts and sails were fitted, and the ship was converted from a schooner to a barquentine. The filthy holds were cleaned, and the living quarters were modified to house the maximum number of men for the expedition.

While the *Nimrod* was being worked on, planning for the expedition moved into high gear. A tiny expedition office was set up on Regent Street in London. Ernest and Emily moved back to the city with two-year-old Raymond and baby Cecily. They rented a house in Bayswater, but Ernest was seldom there. He crisscrossed the country talking to anyone who would lend or give him money for the expedition. Slowly funds trickled in. Ernest also took a three-week trip to Norway, where he talked to experts about the best sledges, clothing, and winter gear for Antarctica and purchased what they recommended. Back in London he met with Fridtjof Nansen, who was now the Norwegian ambassador. Unlike Robert Scott, Fridtjof was willing to help Ernest in any way he could, and the two men spent hours poring over maps and figures.

Before long the tiny expedition office was cluttered with samples of innovative products they might use on the trip. Among these were packing cases made of Venesta, a thin, strong, waterproof and lightweight, three-layer birch plywood. By using Venesta packing cases, Ernest calculated that he could save over four tons in weight. The wood from the empty cases could be reused for all sorts of purposes in Antarctica. Also among the products were a dozen fur sleeping bags and fur boots from Lapland.

Then there was the matter of transportation in Antarctica to consider. Fridtjof insisted that no expedition would make it to the South Pole without using sled dogs. Ernest disagreed. Perhaps that was true for Norwegians, who grew up working with sled dogs, but not for Englishmen. Ernest knew firsthand how wild, undisciplined, and difficult to control the dogs had been on the *Discovery* expedition. Although Ernest decided he would take some sled dogs with him, he intended to rely on Manchurian ponies on the ice. A single pony could pull about twelve hundred pounds of supplies and travel twenty to thirty miles a day. The ponies had been used successfully in the Arctic on the private Jackson-Harmsworth Expedition to Franz Josef Land, or so Ernest had been led to believe. He had already arranged for suitable Manchurian ponies to be purchased in China.

Ernest had another form of transportation that made Fridtjof shake his head as well—an automobile. William Beardmore, one of the expedition's financial backers, manufactured Arrol-Johnston cars. He proposed that Ernest take a specially adapted car to Antarctica—a four-cylinder, fifteen-horsepower, air-cooled vehicle, which William claimed could travel 150 miles over ice in twenty-four hours.

Privately, Ernest didn't expect the car to perform well on the ice, but he was willing to try it out. He decided that the extra attention the British Antarctic Expedition was getting as a result of the vehicle was worth the expense of transporting it south, even if it never drove a mile on the ice.

With several weeks to go before the expedition departed, Ernest turned his attention to recruiting team members. He had initially hoped that many men from the *Discovery* expedition would join him, but that hope had long since faded. He set out to find his own men. Ernest had a different set of priorities than Captain Scott had on the *Discovery*. While he realized that the crewmen needed to be well qualified, Ernest also looked for something else. He wanted team players. He wanted men who got along with others, who were willing to put aside class and rank to pitch in to do whatever was necessary for the sake of the ship and the expedition. If the men were going to spend two years together, it was important to Ernest that they all got along.

One by one, Ernest found his men. The captain was Rupert England, who had been first mate on the *Morning*. There were Bernard Day, a twenty-two-year-old mechanic; Dr. Eric Marshall, the expedition's surgeon; and James Murray, a well-known Scottish biologist. Ernest also managed to get two petty officers from the *Discovery*, Frank Wild and Ernest Joyce, to join the expedition. George Marston, an accomplished artist and friend of two of Ernest's sisters, signed on as the expedition's official artist.

Working almost around the clock, Ernest got the *Nimrod* outfitted for Antarctica. Stores and equipment were stowed in her holds, and a crew was ready to depart by the end of July 1907. On July 30 the *Nimrod* sailed down the Thames and out to sea. Like the *Discovery*, she was inspected by King Edward VII at the regatta at Cowes on the Isle of Wight. Both King Edward and Queen Alexandra came aboard ship, giving the expedition royal approval. In a short ceremony, King Edward pinned the medal of the Royal Victorian Order on Ernest's chest, and the queen surprised Ernest with a silk flag. The note with it read, "May this Union Jack which I entrust to your keeping lead you safely to the South Pole." Ernest certainly hoped it would.

Chapter 10

On the Long Trail

As much as he would have liked to sail on the *Nimrod* to New Zealand, Ernest still had money to raise for the expedition before leaving England. At the end of October, he headed off to join the expedition. He crossed the English Channel, took a train through France, and caught a steamer across the Mediterranean, through the Suez Canal, and on to Australia for a quick visit. Afterward he would travel to New Zealand to meet the ship in Lyttelton.

Ernest arrived in Melbourne, Australia, in early December 1907, only to learn that some of the expedition's financing had fallen through. Undeterred, he pushed on. He gave a public lecture that attracted four thousand people, and he met with one of Australia's leading geologists, Dr. Edgeworth David. Dr. David was nearly fifty years old and interested in exploring potential mineral deposits in Antarctica. Ernest liked him and invited him to join the British Antarctic Expedition, along with two of his past students, Douglas Mawson, a geologist, and Bertram Armytage.

Dr. David immediately applied for a grant from the Australian government for mineral exploration in Antarctica, and the expedition was allocated five thousand pounds. With fresh finances in hand, Ernest, accompanied by the other three men, sailed to New Zealand. Much to Ernest's relief, the New Zealand public had gotten behind the expedition. The Lyttelton Harbour Board waived its docking fees for the *Nimrod* and gave the crew free train passes to nearby Christchurch. Better yet, local newspapers called for the New Zealand government to help fund the expedition. Ultimately, the government gave one thousand pounds.

Every bit of money was needed to finish stocking the ship with everything the fifteen-man wintering-over party would need to survive for a year on the ice. By Ernest's reckoning, 180 tons of supplies would need to be offloaded onto the ice. This included the Arrol-Johnston car, a large iron stove, and the nine Manchurian ponies and nine sled dogs that joined the ship in Lyttelton.

By the time everything was loaded, Ernest had to face the fact that the *Nimrod* could not carry any more cargo across the dangerous Southern Ocean. But the ship still needed about one hundred tons of coal for it to steam to Antarctica and back. Something had to be done, and fast. Ernest came up with a unique plan.

He asked the Union Steamship Company in Dunedin if it could spare its much larger steamer, the *Koonya*, to tow the *Nimrod* to Antarctica. That way, the *Nimrod* wouldn't have to take so much coal, and the *Koonya* could also carry some of the other cargo. The Union Steamship Company's chairman not only agreed to do it but also offered to pay half the cost if the New Zealand government paid the other half. Ernest was relieved when the government agreed to the arrangement. The expedition was back in business.

On New Year's Day 1908, over fifty thousand people packed into Lyttelton to see the *Nimrod* on her way. The little sealer rendezvoused with the *Koonya* outside Lyttelton Harbour. A four-hundred-yard-long, four-inch-diameter steel cable was attached to the *Nimrod*'s bow, and the ship shut down her engine as the bigger ship took her in tow. A storm blew up as the two ships plowed on through mountainous seas. The weight of the towline caused the *Nimrod*'s bow to drag, and the ship, pitching and rolling badly, nosed its way through the waves. Soon most of the crew were seasick, and the ship reeked of vomit.

After fourteen days of discomfort aboard the *Nimrod*, the crew encountered their first iceberg. As they approached the Antarctic Circle, pack ice was visible ahead. This was the signal that the *Koonya* had gone as far as she could go. A boat was lowered over the *Nimrod*'s side, and Captain England took a batch of mail from the crew across to the *Koonya*. He brought back ten freshly butchered sheep, gifts from farmers in New Zealand. The plan was to transport more supplies to the *Nimrod*, but the wind, which whipped into a gale, prevented this. The *Koonya*'s captain let the towline go, came about, and headed north, leaving the *Nimrod* alone to continue under her own steam.

Nine days later the vessel reached the Ross Ice Shelf at a point almost midway between McMurdo Sound to starboard and King Edward VII Land to port. Ernest ordered the captain to turn to port. Even though McMurdo Sound was a much deeper and therefore safer inlet, Ernest was determined to keep his promise to Robert Scott.

The *Nimrod* steamed along the edge of the ice shelf, but the pack ice was thicker than Ernest had anticipated. Because of this, the ship couldn't get close enough to King Edward VII Land to anchor and to set up winter quarters. Ernest had to face the fact that if they were to stay in Antarctica, they needed to head to the best-known inlet, Winter Quarters Bay on Ross Island, where the *Discovery* had anchored. The decision was agonizing. Ernest wrote to Emily, "I have been through a sort of Hell. . . . My conscience is clear but my heart is sore. But I have one comfort that I did my best."

As they headed to McMurdo Sound, Ernest dreaded what the members of the Royal Geographical Society would say about his change of plan, but he had no choice. For the British Antarctic Expedition to go ahead, the *Nimrod* had to be unloaded and sent back to New Zealand by the end of February. Time was running short.

The *Nimrod* arrived at McMurdo Sound on January 29, 1908, only to find the route to Winter Quarters

Bay and Hut Point blocked by the frozen sea. Little could be done but to wait. In the meantime, Ernest ordered all hands on deck to sort cargo and prepare for landing. On the second day of preparations, Aeneas Mackintosh, the *Nimrod*'s second officer and one of the men who was to winter over, was involved in a serious accident. His right eye was injured by a cargo hook. Later that day, the expedition's two surgeons removed his eye while he lay drugged with chloroform on the floor of a cabin. Ernest was sad to learn that the injury would require a long recovery time and that Aeneas would need to return to New Zealand with the *Nimrod*. That same day, one of the ponies had to be shot. It had been badly injured on the voyage south. Another pony had already been killed for the same reason. Ernest knew that they couldn't afford to lose any more ponies, or their hopes of reaching the South Pole would be dashed.

After waiting five days for the ice to clear, Ernest gave up. He decided that the expedition would winter over on the nearest suitable landing place, which was Cape Royds, named after Charles Royds from the *Discovery*. Hut Point was twenty-three miles south. Late on February 3, the *Nimrod* anchored off the cape, ready to begin transferring 180 tons of supplies, including the car and seven remaining ponies, from the ship onto the ice. Each crate or piece of equipment needed to be quickly sledged across the ice to solid ground, lest a piece of ice break off and drift away, taking crucial supplies with it.

Ernest went ashore at Cape Royds and found a suitable site for the crew's new hut. It was about two hundred yards inland on the floor of a level, ice-free valley. The first thing unloaded from the *Nimrod* was the large, prefabricated hut they had brought with them. Once the hut was erected, the rest of the supplies were unloaded from the ship.

February 15 was Ernest's thirty-fourth birthday, but he barely had time to stop for a toast with the ship's crew. He still had much to do. The temperature was dropping, and the *Nimrod* needed to be on her way soon lest she become trapped in the ice.

The backbreaking work of unloading the ship was finished by February 22, when the *Nimrod* steamed away from Cape Royds for New Zealand, leaving fourteen men ashore on Ross Island—the only humans on the entire continent. The men had only each other to depend on as they endured the harsh Antarctic winter and then attempted to reach the South Pole. In England, many of the men, who were from different social classes, would have had no reason to get to know each other. In fact, Philip Brocklehurst, the expedition's twenty-year-old assistant geologist, was actually Sir Philip Brocklehurst, Second Baronet of Swythamley Park, Leek, Staffordshire, while twenty-three-year-old Bernard Day, the electrician and motor mechanic, was from humble roots. On the ice, as far as Ernest was concerned, each person was important, and they all needed each other to survive.

Ernest had hoped to make one journey south before winter fully descended to set up a supply depot in preparation for the South Pole attempt. He needed to cross the sea ice to do this, but the ice that had stopped them from proceeding to Hut Point had been broken up by a gale, and no safe route across the bay was available. Edgeworth David asked to take a party to climb Mount Erebus, the volcano looming above their camp, and Ernest let them go. The volcano would supply the geology team with lots of data and test the men against the harsh elements. If they made it to the top, they would be the first men to climb an Antarctic mountain.

On March 5, 1908, six men set out from the hut. Dr. David and Douglas Mawson, two of the expedition's four geologists, and Dr. Alistair Mackay formed the core of the team. They were accompanied by a supply team made up of Jameson Adams, Philip Brocklehurst, and Dr. Eric Marshall. Eight men, including Ernest, stayed at the hut, where they busied themselves getting their base camp organized. Using Venesta, they lined the hut with shelves and made a dining table that could be hoisted up into the rafters when not in use. From time to time, using a telescope, Ernest would catch a glimpse of six tiny figures ascending the mountain.

Transportation had become a concern, and Ernest secretly wondered if he had done the right thing bringing ponies. Another one had died from eating volcanic sand, leaving only six. And the Arrol-Johnston car had proved totally useless. It was hard to keep it running in the freezing Antarctic climate. When the motor did run, the wheels spun on the ice but the car wouldn't move.

On the morning of March 11, the six men who had climbed Mount Erebus staggered back to Cape

Royds. They were greeted with cheers and an enormous helping of oatmeal, ham, and bread and butter. Ernest was delighted to hear that all but Philip Brocklehurst had made it to the volcano's summit, which they calculated to be 13,370 feet above sea level. The only mishap of the climb was Philip's frostbitten toes. Eric Marshall and Alistair Mackay, the expedition's two surgeons, concurred that Philip's big toe needed to be amputated. Philip, who had turned twenty-one on the slopes of Mount Erebus, took the news stoically.

The morning after the Erebus party returned, another pony died, and two days later still another. Now only four ponies were left, and Ernest knew that even if the last four survived the winter, he would have to reduce the number of men attempting to reach the South Pole.

The team had brought nine dogs from New Zealand, and two litters of puppies had been born on the ice. Another litter had been born on the *Nimrod* on the way south, but Ernest didn't think they would make it all the way to the South Pole. Instead, he planned to use the dogs for the support team that would go partway south with them.

At Cape Royds the men settled in for the long winter. Sometimes a blizzard would rage outside for a week or more. The only time the men left the hut was to relieve themselves or tend the animals housed on the porch. Ernest worked hard making sure the men kept busy and happy. The men had plenty of time to read books aloud, perform plays and skits, and produce a book to commemorate the expedition.

The book was called *Aurora Australis.* Artist George Marston designed the cover, and Frank Wild and Ernest Joyce produced the book on a small printing press, which Ernest had brought south from England for that purpose.

As winter drew to a close, Ernest had to decide who should join him in the attempt to reach the South Pole. Edgeworth David and Douglas Mawson, accompanied by Alistair Mackay, had already asked for permission to venture out in search of the South Magnetic Pole, which they estimated to be about five hundred miles away. Raymond Priestly, one of the other geologists, and Bertram Armytage planned to make a trek to the western mountains for geological research. Two other men were eliminated because of medical issues: Philip's foot was healing slowly, and Ernest Joyce had developed liver problems. Of the remaining seven healthy men, Ernest chose three: Jameson Adams, Eric Marshall, and Frank Wild. Once the spring twilight arrived, all the men took turns ferrying supplies across the iced-over bay to the abandoned hut at Hut Point in preparation for the journey.

Ernest put biologist James Murray in charge until his return. He told James that the *Nimrod,* which would return at the end of summer to collect the expedition members, was to leave by March 1, 1909, at the latest. James was to make sure that the hut at Hut Point was manned around the South Pole party's expected return date, and they were to watch for signals from them. If the South Pole party didn't arrive, James was to leave three men and enough supplies for them all for the winter at Cape Royds before the *Nimrod* departed.

On the night of October 28, 1908, all the plans were in place, and Ernest sat on a box and wrote in his journal. "At last we are on the long trail after 4 years thought and work. I pray that we may be successful for my Heart has been so much in this." The next morning the four men set out for the South Pole.

Chapter 11

Farthest South

The sun shone brightly as the four men crossed the ice to Hut Point. The four surviving ponies, Grisi, Socks, Quan, and Chinaman, pulled loaded sledges behind them. Ernest led the way, guiding Quan by the bridle. Frank, Jameson, and Eric trailed behind with their ponies. In the rear came the support team, man-hauling sledges behind them. By the time they reached Hut Point, twenty miles south, two mishaps had occurred. One of the ponies had become lame, and another had kicked Jameson, cutting his shin to the bone.

Ernest decided that the men and the ponies would rest for three days before resuming the trek south. According to his calculations, the South Pole was 747 miles from their position. He had set an ambitious goal for the group of covering sixteen miles a day. If they kept to that goal, they had enough food to get them to the pole and back. They climbed onto the Ross Ice Shelf, where they encountered drifts of windblown ice. The ponies sometimes sank up to their bellies in them. The pace was slow, and two days into the trek they had to set up camp and wait out a blizzard. Huddled in their sleeping bags, the men took turns reading aloud from the book each had been allowed to bring on the journey. Ernest had chosen William Shakespeare's comedies. He decided they would need something to make them laugh. Forty-eight hours passed before they were on their way again.

The support party turned back on November 7, leaving Ernest and the other three men to go on alone. Before they left, Ernest ordered Ernest Joyce to return and establish an extra supply depot near Minna Bluff, one hundred miles south of Cape Royds, before the group's expected return from the South Pole.

The four men trekked on through a field of fractured ice. Deep crevasses were covered by a thin crust of ice, making the gaps difficult to detect. Ernest led the way, trusting providence to guide him. At one point Chinaman, Frank's pony, fell through the ice, and it took all the men's strength to haul him out. If he had fallen any deeper, he would have taken their cooking fuel and supplies with him. This was a sobering realization, but Ernest knew that there was little they could do but walk on and hope for firmer ice.

On November 15, they laid their first supply depot, Depot A, 140 miles from Cape Royds. Ernest wrote in his journal, "We are but tiny specks in the immensity around us, crawling slowly and painfully across the white plain. Our imaginations take wings until a stumble in the snow, the sharp pangs of hunger, or the dull ache of physical weariness bring back our attention."

The men and ponies trudged on. The weather improved so much they were able to average sixteen miles a day, and Ernest was optimistic about their chances of making it to the South Pole. However, on November 21, twenty-four days after setting out from Cape Royds, the group lost its first member. Chinaman went completely lame and had to be shot. Eric butchered the meat, some of which they cooked. All four men ate until full. The remaining eighty pounds of Chinaman's meat, along with some oil and biscuits, were left to form supply Depot B.

Carrying on with the trek, five days later the men passed the *Discovery* expedition's farthest south record. Ernest thought back six years to 1902 when he had marched south to this point with Robert Scott and Edward Wilson. It had taken them fifty-nine days to reach it, but Ernest and his group had covered the distance in twenty-nine days. Not only that, but Ernest's team was still relatively fit and healthy, even if they had to tighten their belts another notch every few days.

Continuing on through the freezing whiteness surrounding them, the men and ponies suffered from snow blindness. Yet the three remaining ponies continued pulling their sledges. However, conditions on the ice were tough for the animals, and first

Grisi faltered, and then Ernest's pony, Quan. Both ponies had to be put down. Each man began hauling sledges weighed down with 150 pounds of supplies. Socks, the only surviving pony, trudged on, pulling six hundred pounds of supplies on a sledge.

On December 2, the group approached the boundary between the Ross Ice Shelf and the Antarctic mainland. They had covered 440 miles since setting out. Before them stood a formidable barrier, the towering Transantarctic Mountains, which the men did not have the equipment or energy to climb over. Ernest reasoned that there must be a pass through the mountain range. But could they find it in time?

The next day, as the men made their way south along the mountain range, Ernest spotted an opening. They headed for it over broken ice. Soon Ernest was staring at what he called the Highway to the South, a huge glacier running almost due south between two rows of mountains. The glacier stretched to the horizon, rising toward an inland plateau. Ernest named it Beardmore Glacier after William Beardmore, who had helped fund the expedition.

During the next four days as they began to ascend the glacier, the men and Socks picked their way once more around deep crevasses obscured by a thin crust of ice. As he led the way, Ernest heard a yell and looked back to see Frank's sledge balanced at a strange angle. Neither Frank nor Socks was anywhere to be seen. Ernest hurried back and discovered the sledge straddling a deep crevasse, with Frank clinging to its lip with one hand. Ernest pulled him to safety, but there was no hope for Socks. The pony had disappeared into the deep darkness of the fissure. After pulling the sledge to safety, Ernest examined it and discovered that the leather harness had snapped under Socks's weight. If it hadn't, the pony would have dragged the sledge and supplies to the bottom of the crevasse as well, and probably Frank with it.

Losing the last pony was a bitter blow, especially since Ernest had been counting on the meat to eventually help feed them. Instead, they boiled up Socks's maize feed and mixed it with their hoosh. In anticipation of their slower progress, Ernest reduced their rations by half.

Beardmore Glacier was 125 miles long, and its surface kept changing. Sometimes the ice was razor-edged, other times deeply crevassed or deathly smooth. Slowly, bruised and suffering from surface frostbite, the men moved on. They climbed along the center of the glacier, where there seemed to be the least number of obstacles.

The four polar explorers celebrated Christmas 1908 ten thousand feet up on Beardmore Glacier. Ernest produced some reminders of home, including a tiny plum pudding and cocoa. The men relished the treats. After taking a theodolite reading, it was determined that they were 250 miles from the South Pole, but they had only one month's food rations left.

Since they were still behind in the miles covered each day, Ernest decided to cut their rations in half again, but Eric told him that that was not a good idea. Each man's body temperature had dipped two degrees below normal, a sign that their bodies were starting to shut down. The last thing they needed was fewer rations. Given this, Ernest didn't halve the rations again, but he did lower them.

After Christmas they reached the head of the glacier. Before them lay a vast polar plateau.

New Year's Day 1909 passed without a special dinner, and the next day Ernest wrote in his journal, "I cannot think of failure yet I must look at the matter sensibly and consider the lives of those who are with me."

On January 4, 1909, the men sat in their tent discussing the future. None of them wanted to go back, but neither could they go on pulling 150 pounds apiece on sledges. They decided to make another supply depot, leaving as much as possible behind and making a dash for the South Pole.

Over the next two days they struggled against a strong headwind but still managed to cover twenty-five miles. Ernest had high hopes that they would make it to the pole, but the following morning they awoke to the sound of a howling blizzard. They couldn't leave their tent for two days. They broke camp on January 9 and set out again, with about 110 miles to go.

As they marched on, Ernest thought of letting the other men rest while he went on alone to the South Pole. Because he realized that that would put them all at greater risk, he decided that they would stay as a team. They would reach the South Pole together or not at all. It was soon obvious to Ernest that they had gone far enough. The men were weak, hungry, and exhausted, and their food supply was rapidly dwindling. They had reached latitude 88 degrees 23 minutes south. They were just ninety-seven miles from the South Pole. They had gone farther south in Antarctica than anyone else, surpassing Robert Scott's farthest south record by 366 miles. It was a remarkable achievement.

It was now time to head back to McMurdo Sound. Before departing, Ernest named the polar plateau King Edward VII Plateau and claimed it for Great Britain. The men planted the silk Union Jack flag that Queen Alexandra had presented to Ernest. Ernest took a photo of the other three men standing next to it, and then the team headed back.

Ernest knew that they were in a race for their lives and needed to travel as light and as fast as they could. They hauled one sledge behind them. Mercifully, they reached the last supply depot they had set up. Ernest estimated that if they found every depot and didn't encounter blizzards or illness along the way, they could make it back to Cape Royds in time to rendezvous with the *Nimrod.*

The men pushed on back the way they had come, their feet swollen, muscles aching, lips cracked, and eyes plagued by snow blindness. The next supply depot was 180 miles away, and they had only five days of rations left. To stretch them, Ernest cut rations in half. He also fashioned a sail from a tent floor and attached it to the sledge to take advantage of the biting tailwind.

On January 16, stumbling forward, they spotted the Transantarctic Mountains, at the base of which their next food supply depot lay. On they toiled for two more days before reaching the depot. There were fourteen days of short rations at the depot as well as extra clothing and a tent.

After leaving the depot the men climbed onto the head of Beardmore Glacier and began their descent to the Ross Ice Shelf. Sometimes they traveled at a speed of less than a mile per hour, and sometimes the tailwind pushed them forward so that they covered twenty miles or more a day. At still other times they were stranded by blizzards, depleting their meager rations as they waited out the storms in their tents. At last they reached a depot partway down the glacier and replenished their rations. The problem was that their hunger was always greater than the quantity of food laid up at a depot, and they had to stretch those rations to get them to the next depot. So although they collected more rations at each depot, their hunger continued to increase.

The men carried on down the glacier toward the supply depot at the bottom. Ernest and the other three were gaunt and weak, and they were still four hundred miles from Cape Royds. When they made it to the supply depot at the foot of the glacier, they made a boiling pot of hoosh, into which they added some of the pony meat laid up there. It was the first solid food they had eaten in thirty-six hours. They gulped the hoosh down. It tasted delightful to Ernest, but there wasn't enough of it to stave off the hunger pangs he felt or to renew his strength. It seemed just enough to keep him alive.

The men were now off the glacier and back on the barrier ice of the Ross Ice Shelf. As strange as it seemed to Ernest, now that they had climbed down from the bitterly cold, high polar plateau, it actually felt warmer on the ice.

By now Ernest was particularly worried about Frank, the smallest man of the group. Dysentery had struck him, shrinking him down to a mere skeleton. Even on the meanest of rations, Ernest secretly gave one of his biscuits to Frank, who needed every calorie he could get. But things got worse. On February 4, 1909, Ernest wrote in his diary, "Cannot write any more. All down with acute dysentery. Terrible day. Our food lies ahead and death stalks us from behind." It seemed unlikely to Ernest that any of them would be able to muster the strength to leave their tents again, but somehow they managed to rally themselves. Three days later they were on their way.

Thankfully, a combination of oatmeal and biscuits helped Frank regain some of his strength. The men pushed on across the ice and on February 10 reached supply Depot B. Hungry and weak, they dug up the pony liver they had buried there and ate it all. They were still so desperately hungry they made a blood soup, salvaging the frozen blood of the slaughtered pony from the ice. Frank told Ernest it was a "beautiful soup." The food revived the men enough to set their sights on making it to Depot A, about one hundred miles to the north.

As they set out from Depot B, Ernest set their ration quantity based upon what they had collected at the depot. Every day each man got one and a half cups of meat, six biscuits, three spoonfuls of pemmican, a spoonful of sugar, and a mug of weak cocoa. Ernest knew that it was nowhere near enough to replace the calories the men were burning each day in their race against starvation.

By Ernest's calculation, they had 230 miles to go and were currently averaging eight and a half miles a day. If they kept up that pace, they would reach McMurdo Sound on March 9. However, Ernest had left instructions that if they were not back at Hut Point or Cape Royds by March 1, the *Nimrod* was to sail without them. For all Ernest knew, the ship could have already come and gone.

The weather was mild and the ice crisp beneath their feet as they trudged on. Ten days later they arrived at Depot A, where they made a wonderful meal of jam and biscuits before replenishing their rations and moving on.

Two days later, on February 22, they saw their first signs of civilization in almost four months. They spotted footprints and dog paw prints in the snow, and then they came upon a pile of empty food cans. Ernest was elated. He had instructed Ernest Joyce to return with several men and set up an extra supply depot at the foot of Minna Bluff for their return. He deduced from the cans and footprints that they were the remains of one of the supply party's meals. He figured they had most likely traveled a little farther south from the bluff to see if they could spot the returning men. Not only that, in examining the cans, Ernest noticed that they were a different brand from those the *Nimrod* had originally sailed with. This meant that the ship had returned safely with new food supplies.

The thought spurred the men on. That night they camped twelve miles from Minna Bluff and the extra food they desperately needed. In anticipation of reaching the depot the following day, Ernest allowed the men to eat all the remaining food to get their strength up for a dash to the supply depot. He knew this was risky, but they were desperate. That night he wrote in his journal, "If we do not pick up the depot, there will be absolutely no hope for us."

At 6:45 a.m. the men set off. Ernest dragged himself one foot after the other across the ice. At four in the afternoon, Frank spotted the supply depot. Mustering their last ounces of strength, the men made for it. What they found when they arrived was a feast. Ernest Joyce had left them boiled mutton, eggs, and plum pudding, along with more sledging rations. He had also left a note saying that the *Nimrod* had safely arrived off Cape Royds under the command of a new captain, Frederick Evans. The men lit their Primus stove and quickly cooked themselves a meal, after which Ernest experienced a sensation he had almost forgotten—a full stomach.

The group set off again to cover the final distance to Hut Point, where they hoped to rendezvous with the *Nimrod.* Despite their full stomachs, they were still weak, and diarrhea once more afflicted them. Frank was the first to have it. Then Eric began experiencing paralyzing stomach cramps. But the men kept moving until a blizzard stopped their progress. They were confined to their tents for a day waiting it out. The delay frustrated Ernest. It was February 26, and the *Nimrod* was supposed to depart in three days.

As soon as the blizzard cleared, the men set out again and, despite their physical condition, covered twenty-four miles in twenty-one hours. They finally made camp, but Eric's condition had worsened, and he could not go on. Ernest made the decision to leave Eric behind, along with Jameson to care for him. They were thirty miles from Hut Point, and they had thirty-six hours before the *Nimrod* was due to sail. While the two remained behind, Ernest and Frank would make a dash for Hut Point to raise the alarm and then return for their two companions.

Ernest and Frank set out with a sledge containing a small amount of food and two sleeping bags. They staggered forward as fast as they could go. At eleven the next morning, after walking all night, they stopped for food. Ernest also used a mirror to reflect the sun and signal Hut Point, where he had left instructions for men to be on the lookout for such signals. There was no return flash.

With the food gone, the two men left their sledge and sleeping bags to dash the last few miles to the hut. At last the hut at Hut Point emerged before them. But when they reached it, Ernest stopped dead in his tracks. No one was there, despite his ordering that it be manned in anticipation of their arrival. A note was nailed to the window frame. It was from Edgeworth David explaining that everyone from the *Nimrod* was fit and well. The ship would stand off the Glacier Tongue halfway between Hut Point and Cape Royds until February 26.

Today was February 28. Ernest and Frank looked at each other. Ernest knew that they were both thinking the same thing. They hoped that by some miracle the *Nimrod* was still in the area. If it was, they needed to attract the crew's attention—and fast. Ernest's eyes settled on the old meteorological shed at the point. He fumbled in his pocket for matches and tried to set the shed alight as a signal, but his fingers were too thick and numb from the cold to hold the match. Next he tried tying a flag to George Vince's memorial cross on the rise behind the hut. Once more his frozen fingers stopped him. Frank tried too but also gave up in frustration.

Sick with disappointment, Ernest helped Frank pry open the hut door. The two fell to the floor inside utterly spent. With no sleeping bags they wrapped themselves in some old roofing felt and huddled together to stay alive. Despite their exhaustion, neither man slept. In the morning Ernest once more attempted to set the old meteorological shed alight. This time he succeeded. He also found a flare in the hut, which he aimed north and fired. "Let's hope there's someone there to see it, Boss," Frank said.

Chapter 12

Splendid Results

Someone had been watching. Soon after Ernest set off the flare, the *Nimrod* rounded Hut Point. They were saved! Within two hours Ernest and Frank were aboard ship. The *Nimrod*'s crew were full of questions. Most of the men were sure that the polar party had all died, and they were shocked to see Ernest and Frank alive. Ernest explained to them what had happened. After devouring a hearty meal of bacon and fried bread, he led a four-man rescue team to find Eric and Jameson. Frank was too exhausted to go along.

The rescue team reached Eric and Jameson at midday on Tuesday, March 2. The men were both in bad shape. After eating the meal that Ernest cooked for them, they all set off back to the ship. In the early hours of March 4, everyone was safely aboard the

Nimrod. During the previous five days, Ernest had walked nearly one hundred miles with little sleep. He was physically and mentally exhausted. It was time to climb into a clean, warm bunk and rest.

When he awoke, Ernest wanted to know why his orders hadn't been followed. Why was no one manning the hut at Hut Point? Captain Evans explained that the expedition's agent in New Zealand had told him that upon his arrival in Antarctica, he was to take charge of the expedition until Ernest returned. And that is what he did. He knew that the South Pole party had left with ninety-one days' rations. When they didn't show up at the end of that time, he became convinced that they were dead and countermanded Ernest's written orders. Who, he asked, could survive 120 days trekking in such a harsh environment on ninety-one days' rations? Ernest still had many questions about the decision but in the end decided to accept the captain's explanation.

Over the next few days, as the *Nimrod* steamed through the ice and away from McMurdo Sound, Ernest learned how the other exploration teams had fared. Edgeworth David, Douglas Mawson, and Alistair Mackay had reached the South Magnetic Pole, along the way collecting many interesting geological specimens. Raymond Priestly and Bertram Armytage had been able to conduct useful geologic research in the western mountains. Although the British Antarctic Expedition had not reached the South Pole, Ernest was proud of his men. They had worked together and surmounted unbelievable obstacles, and not one expedition member had died in the process.

On Tuesday, March 23, 1909, the *Nimrod* was off the coast of Stewart Island at the bottom of New Zealand's South Island. The place looked like paradise to Ernest. It had been thirteen months since he had seen a blade of grass or a wildflower.

The ship's first port of call was the tiny town of Oban on Stewart Island. Ernest sent a coded message to Emily, letting her know that he was alive. Then, as arranged before he left England, he telegraphed a twenty-five-hundred-word story to the *Daily Mail* newspaper in London. The story heralded the expedition's safe arrival from Antarctica and highlighted their successes. He knew that the newspaper would carry the story in its next edition, and the world would soon know what had been achieved.

From Oban the ship sailed to Lyttelton, arriving two days later. Sure enough, word of the expedition's success had already reached the port. A large flag-waving crowd greeted the *Nimrod* as she entered the harbor. Ernest waved to the crowd as the ship docked. In Lyttelton, Ernest received a personal telegraph from the king congratulating him for his achievements and the expedition's "splendid results."

Following the enthusiastic welcome in Lyttelton, New Zealand Prime Minister Joseph Ward hosted a special luncheon and a thanksgiving service in Ernest's honor at nearby Christchurch. Ernest also gave a lecture there, and three thousand people came to hear him. Once more the Lyttelton Port Authority provided the *Nimrod* free berth as repairs were carried out before she sailed back to England. It was time for the men of the British Antarctic Expedition to begin saying goodbye as they went their separate ways. Dr. David and Douglas Mawson headed back to Australia. Ernest went to Wellington, New Zealand's capital, for more receptions and speeches. When he spoke of the expedition, he always talked about his team and how they had gotten as far as they had by all working together.

On April 16, 1909, Ernest left New Zealand for Australia amid a flurry of flags and cheers. He took with him a young New Zealand journalist named Edward Saunders. After seeing the reaction of the New Zealand public to his speeches about the expedition, Ernest suspected that the British public would want a full accounting of the expedition as soon as possible. He hired Edward to help him shape and write a book-length account, hoping the manuscript would be ready for publishing by the time they reached England.

In Australia Ernest received the same rousing welcome he'd had in New Zealand. Again there were receptions and speeches. From Australia he booked passage on the ocean liner *India*, which took him and Edward through the Suez Canal. In Brindisi, Italy, they caught a train to Calais, France, where they crossed to England by ferry. Along the way the two men worked on the book.

Given the enthusiastic welcome in New Zealand and Australia, Ernest anticipated that he would be in demand once he arrived back in London. He told several newspaper reporters that he would arrive late on the afternoon of June 14 at London's Charing Cross station on the "boat train," which carried ferry passengers from Dover into the city. In fact, he arrived in Dover two days before to rest and spend time with his wife, whom he hadn't seen in a year and a half.

At the appointed hour, Ernest appeared at Charing Cross station on the boat train. He had expected a warm welcome, but even he was astonished by just how many people showed up to welcome him home. The station was jammed. In fact, the police had closed the station gates in an attempt to control the enormous crowd, but Ernest didn't disappoint those who couldn't get in. He rode from the station in an open horse-drawn cab, standing and waving and acknowledging the throng outside the station as Emily sat quietly beside him.

A photo of Ernest standing in the open cab amid the crowd and the story of his arrival in London were on the front page of all the newspapers the following day. The newspapers were particularly impressed by the fact that Ernest had gone within ninety-seven miles of the South Pole and returned without losing a man. Not only that, but he had supplied, funded, and organized the British Antarctic Expedition independent of any government help. He was lauded as a self-made man.

Although the public applauded his achievement, Ernest discovered that not everyone appreciated his success. Sir Clements Markham and Robert Scott were less than impressed with his accomplishments and spread rumors that Ernest's latitude readings were false. Neither man could believe that an officer from the merchant marine and his motley expedition crew could outshine the British Navy. Ernest submitted all of his paperwork and calculations to the Royal Geographical Society, who studied them and confirmed that his readings and calculations were accurate. He had indeed gone as far south as he said.

Throughout 1909 accolades continued to roll in for Ernest. In July King Edward VII awarded him the Commander of the Royal Victorian Order, one step down from a knighthood. The following month, the British government offered to pay off the remaining debt of the British Antarctic Expedition. Then in September, the king summoned Ernest to Balmoral Castle in Scotland to spend the weekend with the royal family and give them a private lecture on Antarctica. Ernest felt that King Edward and Queen Alexandra enjoyed his company, and the king asked many insightful questions during the lecture and lantern slide show.

Soon after Ernest's return to London from Balmoral, Robert Scott announced that he was planning another expedition to Antarctica to attempt to reach the South Pole. The news immediately made Ernest consider another expedition there himself. Although he had told Emily on his arrival home that he was done with expeditions to Antarctica, and despite the hardships he had endured on the trip south, he still dreamed of being the first man to reach the South Pole.

Ernest didn't have much time to dwell on such thoughts. He was off to Scandinavia on a lecture tour, where he spoke at many gatherings and met privately with men who had gone south themselves.

He was particularly delighted to meet once again with Roald Amundsen. The two had struck up a friendship several years before in England.

Ernest arrived back in England just in time for the publication of his book on the British Antarctic Expedition. *The Heart of the Antarctic* was immediately made available in seven languages.

The whirlwind of places and events continued. Then in November 1909, Ernest received a surprise. He was knighted by King Edward VII. At thirty-five years of age he became Sir Ernest Shackleton, and his wife was known as Lady Emily.

Ernest was also invited to his old school, Dulwich College, to hand out prizes to the top students. During the speech he gave there, he joked with the students that this was "the nearest I have ever got to a prize."

The tours continued. Ernest started off in 1910 visiting Ireland and the European Continent, where the czar of Russia and the kaiser of Germany welcomed him. Then in March he traveled to the United States with Emily and her sister Daisy on a lecture tour. He was in Chicago on May 6, 1910, when news came that King Edward VII had died. His forty-four-year-old son became King George V. Ernest was saddened by the news. He had liked King Edward VII and felt that he had taken a genuine and intelligent interest in Antarctic exploration.

Soon after returning from the United States, Ernest went to Robert Scott's farewell. Robert's expedition, traveling aboard the ship *Terra Nova*, was going to try for the South Pole. As before, Scott's expedition had the backing of the Royal Geographical Society and the government.

Robert Scott was not the only one with an eye on being the first man to the South Pole. Wilhelm Filchner, the German polar explorer, was preparing to take an expedition to Antarctica with plans of reaching the South Pole. A Japanese expedition was already on its way to Antarctica with instructions to reach the South Pole or die trying. Then, unexpectedly, there was another contender. On October 4, 1910, news broke that Roald Amundsen had secretly sailed south to Antarctica and was preparing an attempt to reach the South Pole. Ernest wished that he could go south with them.

As 1911 dawned, Ernest looked back over the previous year. He had traveled over twenty thousand miles and addressed more than a quarter of a million people. Yet he felt restless. More than anything he wanted to be back on the ice in the race for the South Pole. But he felt he had to stay home. Emily needed him. At forty-three years of age, she had just learned that she was expecting another baby, due in the middle of the year. Ernest knuckled down and tried his hardest to be a homebody with his wife and children. On July 15, 1911, Emily gave birth to another son, whom they named Edward. Ernest was now the father of two sons and a daughter.

As 1911 wore on, Ernest waited anxiously for word of Robert Scott's and Roald Amundsen's expeditions. News came on March 7, 1912, when the newspapers blazed the headline, "Amundsen Reached South Pole on 14 December 1911." The story under the headline told how Roald Amundsen had led a team of four other men and sixteen sled dogs and had arrived at latitude 90 degrees zero minutes south—the South Pole.

Since Ernest had expected one of the expeditions would make it to the pole, he was not too surprised at the news. He sent a telegram to Roald: "Heartiest congratulations magnificent achievement." And in a letter to the British people published in the *Daily Chronical*, Ernest urged the country to applaud Roald's magnificent accomplishment: "The same endurance, the same skill and the same need of endeavour must be granted to Amundsen, as the Norwegian people would grant to Scott if the positions [were] reversed."

While Ernest encouraged the English to look beyond national pride and give Roald Amundsen the respect he deserved for being the first man to the South Pole, the country waited anxiously for news of Robert Scott and his expedition. It did not come for another eleven months. In February 1913, news broke that a search party had found three bodies frozen to death in the ice: Robert Scott, Ernest's old friend Edward Wilson, and Henry Bowers.

Scott's recovered journal told the rest of the story. Five members of the expedition had reached the South Pole on January 17, 1912, five weeks after Amundsen, but on their return, one of them, Edgar Evans, dropped dead from exhaustion. Another, Lawrence Oates, with his hands and feet useless from frostbite, walked away from the tent never to return. Scott, Wilson, and Bowers struggled on, but a fierce blizzard halted their advance. They knew they were only ten miles from a supply depot, but weakened and suffering from frostbite, they died in their tent before weather conditions improved enough for them to reach the depot.

The British public took pride in Scott's achievement in reaching the South Pole and were saddened by the men's deaths. Ernest was more interested in reading Scott's journals to discover what had gone wrong and what he could do better. Both the North and South Poles had now been reached. As far as Ernest was concerned, only one great polar feat remained—crossing Antarctica from one side to the other via the South Pole.

Over the next several months Ernest began planning an expedition to do just that. He set up the new expedition's office at 4 New Burlington Street, London, among a row of fabric shops and drapers. He planned to take two ships and two separate parties. One ship would travel to the Vahsel Bay area on the Weddell Sea side of Antarctica, where fourteen men would land. Six of them, under Ernest's leadership, would then set out on the eighteen-hundred-mile journey across Antarctica to the Ross Sea. The other ship would sail to McMurdo Sound, from where men would head inland and lay supply depots as far as Beardmore Glacier along the route the transcontinental party would follow. That ship would then transport both parties home from McMurdo Sound. The plan was ambitious, but Ernest was sure that with the right men and equipment it could be successful. He named the venture the Imperial Trans-Antarctic Expedition.

Now that he had a plan, Ernest needed to cobble together the money from a variety of sources to fund the expedition. He approached the Royal Geographical Society, but they were not willing to sponsor the expedition. They did give him one thousand pounds toward financing it. Ernest's old friend Hugh Mill refused to even talk to him about the plan. He thought the whole expedition was a death trap. But Ernest was persistent, and ultimately several rich people stepped forward to help fund the venture. Among them were Scottish industrialist Sir James Caird, manufacturer Dudley Docker, heiress Janet Stancomb-Wills, Lord Iveagh, Sir Robert Lucas-Tooth, Elizabeth Dawson-Lambton, and playwright J. M. Barrie, author of *Peter Pan.* The British government offered him ten thousand pounds, and the *Daily Chronicle* bought the rights to the news and pictures from the expedition.

In early January 1914, Ernest purchased two ships. The first was the *Polaris,* a new, three-hundred-ton wooden barquentine built in Norway for polar exploration. The original buyer had been unable to pay for the ship, and Ernest quickly snapped it up. It was the perfect vessel for the Weddell Sea party, which Ernest would lead. He renamed the ship *Endurance,* after his family's motto. The second ship was the *Aurora,* which had just returned to Australia following Douglas Mawson's Australasian Antarctic Expedition. Ernest asked to purchase the *Aurora* for use by the Ross Sea party. Douglas sold it to him for thirty-two hundred pounds.

Now that he had ships, Ernest needed personnel to sail them. He made an announcement in the newspapers about the expedition. He was not prepared for the avalanche of interest that descended upon him. Newspaper reporters stood at the door of his office waiting for him to arrive in the morning, and hundreds of applications to join the expedition poured in.

Because Ernest valued loyalty more than anything else, he reached out to those with whom he had been on previous expeditions. Much to his delight, a strong team quickly formed. Frank Wild showed up in person to apply. He had just returned from being a part of Douglas Mawson's expedition. Ernest signed his old friend on immediately as second-in-command. Frank would sail on the *Endurance* with Ernest. Also assigned to the *Endurance* was Alfred Cheetham, who had been third officer on the *Nimrod* and bosun of Robert Scott's *Terra Nova.* George Marston returned as the expedition's official artist. Tom Crean was chosen for second officer. He had been on the *Discovery* expedition with Ernest and had also been on the *Terra Nova* expedition. He was the man who had found Robert Scott's body frozen in his tent on the ice. Able seaman Thomas McLeod, who had also been on the *Terra Nova,* was also signed on. While these men all had Antarctic experience, Ernest kept adding to the *Endurance*'s crew from among those who applied who had never been south. To captain the *Endurance,* he chose Frank Worsley, a merchant marine officer from New Zealand.

Not only did Ernest need a seasoned crew to sail the *Endurance,* but also he needed scientists and other personnel. Among them were James Wordie, a geologist, and Reginald James, a physicist, both from Cambridge University.

While filling positions on the *Endurance* party, Ernest was assigning men to the *Aurora* party. Among them was Aeneas Mackintosh, *Nimrod*'s second officer who had lost an eye in an accident aboard. He would be the *Aurora*'s captain. Ernest Joyce, an able seaman on the *Discovery* who was also on the *Nimrod* expedition, joined the Ross Sea party. He, too, had recently returned from Douglas Mawson's expedition. Ernest Wild, Frank Wild's brother, a petty officer in the Royal Navy, would also serve on the *Aurora*. Ernest knew that Frank and his brother were cut from the same loyal and dependable cloth.

Part of Ernest's plan to cover the cost of the expedition was to sell the photos and a movie. To make this possible, he asked Frank Hurley to join the expedition as photographer/cinematographer. Frank was an Australian who had been the photographer on the Australasian Antarctic Expedition. Ernest was impressed by the quality of his photographs. Frank immediately accepted Ernest's invitation and arranged to travel from Australia to Buenos Aires, Argentina, to join the *Endurance* when she docked there on the way to Antarctica.

As Ernest kept busy organizing the details of the expedition, an unexpected visitor appeared at his office on New Burlington Street—Roald Amundsen. The two men sat down for a private meeting and went over Ernest's expedition plans. Roald was adamant that Ernest use dog teams, not horses, to pull the sleds, and that the men use skis instead of walking. Ernest, who had the greatest admiration for the polar explorer, took his advice. He promptly ordered sled dogs from Canada which would be taken aboard the *Endurance* in Buenos Aires.

Originally Ernest hoped that the Royal Navy would pay for and man the *Aurora*, but that didn't work out. Because tensions were rising in Europe that could draw Great Britain into war, the navy could spare neither the men nor the money. One day, Captain Thomas Orde-Lees, a Royal Marine, roared up to the expedition office on a motorbike. Ernest was impressed, since few people rode motorbikes. Thomas told him that he wanted to join the expedition. He was a skier and a mountain climber and liked to tinker with engines. Currently he was superintendent of physical training at a Royal Marine Depot School. This was a combination of skills Ernest could not resist. He took Thomas to see Winston Churchill, First Lord of the Admiralty, and asked him to loan Captain Orde-Lees to the expedition. Churchill agreed, and Ernest had another member for the crew.

Having met with cooperation from the navy, Ernest approached the War Office for a different reason. Colonel Wilfred Beveridge was an Army nutritional expert, and Ernest wanted his help in planning the best possible diet for his men. Two years earlier, vitamins had been discovered, and Ernest, with the colonel's help, was eager to make use of this new knowledge. Ernest also wanted to make use of another recent food innovation—food dehydration—that would save much weight as the men crossed Antarctica hauling their food rations with them.

In early summer, Ernest and eight members of the expedition traveled to Norway to test out a new motorized sledge and the reformulated rations that Wilfred Beveridge had recommended. The food tasted good, but Ernest had doubts about the motor on the sledge having enough horsepower to be of much use.

On Saturday, August 1, 1914, the *Endurance* sailed from the West India Docks on the Thames. This was a more subdued send-off than that of the *Nimrod.* Great Britain seemed to be poised on the edge of war. Ernest stayed aboard the *Endurance* until she reached Eastbourne, where he disembarked. He would join the ship in Buenos Aires in September. In the meantime he had financial ends to tie up.

Three days later, on August 4, war went from a possibility to a reality when Great Britain declared war on Germany. Ernest immediately offered the Admiralty his services, along with those of the *Endurance* and her crew. It felt wrong to go exploring when his country needed him. The Admiralty telegraphed Ernest and told him to proceed as planned. The expedition was free to leave. Too much planning and money had gone into it to turn back now.

Ernest said goodbye to Emily and their three children and set out for Buenos Aires. He hoped that news of his transantarctic success would buoy the spirits of the British people and make them proud.

Chapter 13

Summer Had Forgotten the Weddell Sea

When he got to Buenos Aires, Ernest learned that three crew members, including the cook, had been disorderly on the voyage from England. He dismissed them, replacing the cook with Charles Green, a baker from a passenger ship docked in Buenos Aires. He also hired able seaman William Bakewell, who had been stranded when his previous ship sank off Uruguay. Although an American, William told Ernest that he was a Canadian to up his chance of being hired onto a British ship. Frank Hurley, the Australian photographer, and Frank Wild also came aboard, along with the sixty sled dogs Ernest had ordered from Canada. The dogs were loaded into kennels built on the deck by Henry "Chippy" McNish, the *Endurance*'s Scottish carpenter and shipwright. McNish's cat, Mrs. Chippy, who despite the name was a tomcat, was also aboard. He was an excellent rat catcher and the ship's mascot.

More supplies were taken aboard the *Endurance,* and on October 26, 1914, she set sail from Buenos Aires for South Georgia and then Antarctica. Once more Ernest was "the Boss."

The ship was three days at sea when the Boss learned that a stowaway was aboard. Perce Blackborow, an eighteen-year-old from Wales, was found hiding in a locker. Ernest soon learned that Perce was a friend of William Bakewell. The two had been stranded together in Buenos Aires. Ernest remembered that Perce had applied for a seaman's job on the *Endurance* and been turned down. Ernest had thought him too young to take to Antarctica. Now Ernest learned that William and another crew member, Ernest How, had smuggled Perce aboard because they believed that the *Endurance* was undermanned. It was a serious challenge to Ernest's authority, and he considered how to deal with the situation. There was no way to send Perce back, and Ernest had to admit that he admired the boy's pluck and determination. He decided to give Perce a stern talking to and then let him sign on to the crew.

Ernest met Perce beside the locker he had stowed away in. Perce was too sick from hunger and seasickness to stand up. Ernest gave him permission to sit while he told him off. Then, putting his face close to Perce's, he said quietly, "Do you know that on these expeditions we often get very hungry, and if there is a stowaway available he is the first to be eaten?"

The scrawny Welsh boy replied, "They'd get a lot more meat off you, Sir!" Ernest hid a smile.

Ernest assigned Perce to quarters in the fo'c'sle with the seamen and sent him to work as a steward, assisting the cook and serving meals.

The ice-covered peaks of South Georgia emerged over the horizon on November 5. The island was one of the most remote outposts in the British Empire. Surprisingly, most of South Georgia's residents were Norwegians who manned the whaling stations dotted along the bays of the northern coast. The *Endurance* dropped anchor in King Edward Cove off the whaling station of Grytviken, surrounded by steep mountains that hemmed the whaling station against the bay. Despite the mountain grandeur surrounding it, Grytviken was a squalid place. The air was rife with the stench of decomposing whales, and the water of the bay was dirty brown from the animals' blood. On the surface floated guts, grease, and whale carcasses with the blubber stripped from them. The blubber was rendered into oil onshore and shipped to England and South America for use as a lubricant or for making soap and margarine.

Ernest planned to stop at South Georgia for just a few days before sailing on to Antarctica, but the whalers urged him to stay longer. They couldn't remember the pack ice ever being so far north this time of year. They advised Ernest to stay until the warmer summer weather began breaking up the ice. Despite wanting to get to Vahsel Bay as soon as possible, Ernest took their advice.

Ernest encouraged his crew to keep active while they waited. One group of men helped Frank Hurley haul his heavy camera and photographic equipment to the tops of the surrounding peaks, where Frank took stunning pictures across South Georgia. In the photos he shot of the bay below, the *Endurance* was a speck anchored in the middle of it.

Meanwhile Thomas Orde-Lees skied alone on the snow and tinkered with the motor sledge to be used on the ice in Antarctica.

The dogs were released from their kennels to run around, and they gorged themselves each day on discarded whale meat.

During the stay, the Boss was taken by boat on a tour of some of the other whaling stations on the island, among them Husvik, Stromness, and Leith, all located on Stromness Bay. At the whaling stations he met the managers and talked with them about their business. He learned that South Georgia was one hundred miles long and twenty miles wide at its widest point. And although its coast had been charted, almost nothing was known of the island's mountainous interior. No one had ever been there. No one had ever crossed the island overland. Gazing up at row after row of razor-sharp mountains, Ernest could see why.

Before the *Endurance* left, Ernest was able to purchase on credit from the whaling station managers sugar, flour, tinned butter, extra coal, and an extra supply of cold-weather clothing.

On December 5, 1914, after a month anchored off Grytviken, the *Endurance* set sail. The height of summer was approaching, and Ernest felt that the pack ice would have opened up by now, allowing them to cross the Weddell Sea to Vahsel Bay and put ashore the expedition's fourteen-man ground party.

Three days after leaving South Georgia, the *Endurance* encountered ice. Huge chunks of it rubbed and jostled against the ship's side. Ernest realized that the whalers on South Georgia hadn't been exaggerating. The ship was still six hundred miles from the nearest Antarctic coast and already surrounded by ice, and they hadn't yet crossed the Antarctic Circle.

Slowly Frank Worsley, or the Skipper, as everyone called him, guided the ship forward. Often Ernest stood at the bow or climbed to the crow's nest to spot leads of open water amid the ice and guide the Skipper to them. It was slow going, and as Christmas approached, the *Endurance* had still not crossed the Antarctic Circle.

The crew celebrated Christmas 1914 with a dinner of turtle soup, whitebait, canned rabbit, plum pudding, fruit mince pies, and figs. They ate heartily as the *Endurance* bumped her way south amid the ice. But as he celebrated, Ernest was quietly worried. It was as though summer had forgotten the Weddell Sea. The temperature was far colder than normal and the pack ice dense. Ernest had reckoned that they would be at the Antarctic coast by the end of December. Now he realized that this was unrealistic. In fact, it wasn't until New Year's Eve that the ship crossed the Antarctic Circle. At midnight the men toasted the arrival of the new year and sang "Auld Lang Syne," the dogs howling in the background.

Sometimes the *Endurance* would have to sail west as they sought more leads that would allow them to travel south. The journey was slow and laborious. Although Ernest appeared calm on the surface, inside he was anxious. By now they should be approaching Vahsel Bay, not picking their way through heavy sea ice.

Around the *Endurance* the open leads of sea teemed with life. Fat seals lay in the sun on the ice; emperor penguins, looking as though they were wearing tuxedos, bowed to the ship as it passed; and Adélie penguins made a raucous noise from their perches on icebergs. Humpback and killer whales broke the surface with large spouts from their blowholes. In the frigid air above, petrels circled, squawking as they swooped down to grab any scraps thrown overboard. Sometimes, as the Boss looked across the white expanse, it seemed to him that the ice was on fire, with smoke rising from it. He was actually seeing frost smoke, a fog formed as frigid air flowed over patches of open water in the ice.

January was the height of the Antarctic summer, and the sun never set. The constant daylight helped with navigating the ice, making treacherous icebergs easy to spot and avoid. A collision with one of them could sink the *Endurance.*

Sometimes, when there were no open leads to follow through the ice or when fog closed in around the ship and they could not proceed, Ernest would order the *Endurance* to be moored alongside an ice floe. The crew would go onto the ice and exercise. They particularly liked playing soccer and even in the chilly environment would work up a good sweat. The dogs were also taken from their kennels and let loose on the ice. They barked and bounded after penguins.

It was during one of these stops that the Boss ordered the motorized sledge hauled out of the hold and lowered onto the ice. Thomas Orde-Lees started it up and took it for a run. It was soon obvious to Ernest and the rest of the crew who watched with amusement that the contraption was totally useless on the ice. Whatever it was supposed to do in theory, there was no way it would be useful to the men to help tow their sledges on the overland trek across Antarctica. They would have to rely solely on the dogs to pull their sledges.

By January 19, 1915, the *Endurance* was trapped in the ice. Ernest scoured the pack ice from the crow's nest. He could see no open leads of water in any direction. No matter that it was summer, the *Endurance* was marooned in the ice of the Weddell Sea, one hundred miles from the Antarctic coast. The ship and the members of the Imperial Trans-Antarctic Expedition would have to wait out fall and winter trapped in pack ice and try again to reach Vahsel Bay and begin their overland crossing of Antarctica in the spring, when the pack ice began to break up.

Chapter 14

Crushed Beyond All Hope

Now that they were stuck in the ice, the sailors didn't have much to do. However, the scientists kept busy conducting experiments and collecting specimens, and Frank took photographs. He even hauled his cumbersome camera high into the ship's rigging to capture vast panoramas of the surrounding pack ice.

Ernest noted that the busiest man aboard was Charles Green, the cook, assisted by Perce Blackborow. They provided the expedition members three meals a day, plus tea and a snack in the afternoon. The cook also kept busy butchering the seals and penguins that were shot on the ice and brought aboard to supplement their diet. The seal meat was a dark-red color and when cooked tasted a little like liver. Penguin tasted like beef, codfish, and duck mixed together. Some of the men complained about having to eat such meat but soon got used to it, especially when it was roasted with potatoes and onions.

At midnight on Wednesday, February 17, 1915, the sun dipped below the horizon for the first time. Ernest knew that this was the first sign that fall was approaching. The Antarctic winter wouldn't be far behind.

The *Endurance*'s boilers had been kept fired while she was stuck in the ice, in case a lead opened up and the ship needed to get under way quickly. Keeping the boilers stoked used up half a ton of coal a day, and in March, certain that there would be no more leads until spring, the Boss gave orders to extinguish the boilers. Now, with no hope of escape, serious work was begun to prepare for the cold, dark winter ahead. Ernest sent groups of men out to hunt more seals and penguins. The meat was stored to feed the men and the dogs.

The dogs were relocated onto the ice beside the *Endurance*. Several men constructed "dogloos." The walls were made of stacked blocks of ice sawed into brick shapes, over which frozen sealskins were laid and snow piled on top for a roof. Long wires were run along the several rows of dogloos to which the dogs were chained. Despite all the work, Ernest noted that the dogs preferred sleeping outside in the snow rather than in their dogloos. The dogs were divided into six sledge-pulling teams, with an expedition member as the driver in charge of each team. The drivers exercised their dogs regularly, harnessing them to sledges and racing them across the ice.

The temperature outside sometimes dropped to minus twenty-four degrees Fahrenheit. With the boilers idle, the temperature on the ship dropped fast. Ernest set about establishing a cozy environment for the crew, particularly the officers and other personnel who lived in the deckhouse cabins, where it was now extremely cold. He gave orders for the storage space between decks to be cleared. This space was much more insulated and isolated from the bitter weather outside. Chippy set to work building six-by-five-foot cubicles in the space that would each house two men. A long table was placed down the middle of the passageway, and a freestanding coal-burning stove was installed at one end. When the carpenter was finished, the men moved in and named their cozy new winter quarters The Ritz.

The entire ship's crew ate at the long table, but the sailors continued living in the fo'c'sle below deck at the front of the ship. This space was also insulated and had its own coal stove.

With his men cooped up aboard, Ernest knew that he had to keep them active and focused, lest they go crazy with cabin fever. He made sure that a routine was kept, that meals were served on time, and that the men took care of various chores between meals. He also made sure that the men had plenty of social activities to fill their time and to break the monotony of life stuck in the ice, especially now that the polar night was approaching. There were card games, chess and checkers, and guessing games; group singing, accompanied by Leonard Hussey, the meteorologist, on his banjo; and all kinds of talent shows.

The men even held a contest to discover who was the worst singer aboard. Ernest wasn't surprised when he won the dubious honor. He had never been able to carry a tune.

On Sunday nights the men gathered in The Ritz to listen to gramophone records and sometimes view a lantern slide presentation. Some of the men read aloud to the others to fill the time.

Meanwhile, driven by the Weddell Sea current below, the whole ice pack was moving in a clockwise direction, taking the *Endurance* with it. When the sky was clear enough before the sun had set for the final time that winter, the Skipper used his sextant to determine the sun's angle above the horizon. With that, and the exact time the reading was taken, he calculated the *Endurance*'s position and plotted it on a chart of the Weddell Sea. Ernest assured the men that they were moving steadily north. When they reached warmer water to the north, the ice pack would break up and free the ship. They just had to be patient. It was only a matter of time. In the meantime, they were safe on the *Endurance*. The ship was constructed from the toughest wood available to withstand the pressure of ice against her hull.

Tuesday, June 22, 1915, was Midwinter's Day, the point when, a bit farther north, the days would now start to get longer. Being stuck south of the Antarctic Circle, the men had experienced the twilight and darkness of the polar night for a month already. But they knew that the next time they would see the sun rise was only another month away.

To celebrate the occasion, Ernest held a party. As usual there was a lot of singing and dressing up, and at midnight Charles served a meal of fried bread and onions. The party ended with a toast and everyone singing "God Save the King."

In mid-July a howling blizzard engulfed the *Endurance.* Ernest gave orders that no one leave the ship during the storm except to feed the dogs. And the dogs had a half pound of lard each added to their meals to help them withstand the cold. A wire was strung from the ship to the dogloos so that the men could find their way to and from the ship.

On the *Endurance* the men huddled around the coal stoves. It was the watchman's job to keep all the stoves going. Despite the frigid conditions, Charles and Perce kept busy in the galley preparing meals. During the blizzard, Ernest and the crew began hearing something they hadn't heard until now—the creaking of the timbers of the ship's hull as ice pressed against her sides. The sound frightened Ernest, who was well aware of the power of the ice. In his cabin one night he voiced his concern to Frank Worsley. The Skipper listened carefully and replied, "If we have to leave the ship behind, we'll get by somehow."

"If we do have to, we'll hang on as long as possible," Ernest said. "It's difficult enough for the men as it is without needing to worry about not having the ship for shelter against blizzards and the bitter cold."

Frank nodded.

When the blizzard abated, Ernest ventured up on deck. He was shocked at the havoc the storm had created. In the gloom of oil lights from the ship, he marveled at how the relatively flat ice plain around the vessel had been broken up and jostled about so that now huge, jagged ice slabs jutted into the air, with great drifts of windblown snow piled up behind them. The various ice chunks jostled and scraped together. It was an ominous sight.

Soon afterward, in the polar darkness, Frank Hurley carried his camera onto the ice. He set it up, along with twenty flashes, and took a photograph of the *Endurance.* To Ernest the image he captured was haunting. The forlorn ship was set against a black sky and was now completely white, frozen beneath a layer of ice.

On Monday, July 26, the crew let out a hearty cheer as the sun broke above the horizon. Ernest immediately noticed a change in the men. Hope returned to them, and more so when, at the beginning of August, the ice pressure against the *Endurance*'s sides eased, and with it the terrifying creaking of the vessel's hull.

Throughout August the crew remained in good spirits. Spring wasn't far off, when the ice pack would start breaking up, freeing the ship and letting the expedition get under way once again. Escape for the *Endurance* wasn't to be that easy, however. During the night of August 31, Ernest awoke to the sound of the groaning and creaking of hull timbers. For three days the ice squeezed tight around the ship before easing up. This pattern played out over and over throughout September.

As spring approached the days grew longer and the temperature rose. Cracks in the ice began opening around the ship, but she was far from being free. Nevertheless, the dogs were brought back aboard in case cracks opened up under the dogloos.

The ice continued to pressure the *Endurance* into October, causing her to shake and creak. Ernest hoped that she would hold up, but he had his doubts. He had told the Skipper, "What the ice gets, the ice keeps," and by now he thought the ice was going to keep the *Endurance.* As a result, he consulted with Frank Wild and the Skipper about what to do if the ship was lost. They discussed the situation for a long time before deciding on a plan. They were now drifting in the ice up the Antarctic Peninsula. If the *Endurance* was crushed, they would take to the ice and walk to the northwest, dragging the lifeboats with them. When they reached open water, they would use the boats to make for Paulet Island at the tip of the peninsula. On the island was a stone hut in which the crew of the *Antarctic* had wintered after their vessel sank in 1903. Ernest knew that the Argentines stocked the hut with emergency stores.

On Friday, October 23, the *Endurance* started leaking as her hull planks bent and twisted under the ice pressure. In the boiler room, crewmen took turns at the pumps to keep the water out. Ernest ordered the lifeboats and various pieces of equipment and stores to be transferred onto the ice beside the ship. The dogs also were once more moved onto the ice.

Throughout the night and all the next day, the ship groaned and shuddered as the ice pressed against her. The *Endurance*'s sternpost was ripped away, and her keel was sheared off. Now the decks started buckling, and one by one the beams began snapping. Water flowed into the ship, weighing down the bow. The tired crew continued feverishly pumping the water out. At five o'clock on Wednesday, October 27, 1915, the Boss told them to stop. There was no point in going on. Ernest's worst fear was realized: the *Endurance* had lost the battle, and the ice was going to keep her. "She's going, boys. I think it's time to get off," he told the crew calmly.

Once everyone was off the ship, Ernest walked around to inspect her. The *Endurance* was a mass of snapped and tangled rigging and broken timber. He ordered the exhausted men to erect tents beside the pile of stores and equipment. It was time for the men to get their first night's sleep on the ice.

The following morning Ernest wrote in his journal, "Though we have been compelled to abandon the ship, which is crushed beyond all hope of ever being righted, we are alive and well, and we have stores and equipment for the task that lies before us. The task is to reach land with all the members of the expedition." It was time to put the survival plan into action and head for Paulet Island, 346 miles to the northwest.

Chapter 15

Ocean Camp

Ernest dropped his gold cigarette case and a handful of coins onto the ice and picked up the ship's Bible. He opened it and read aloud from the book of Job, chapter thirty-eight, verses twenty-nine and thirty: "Out of whose womb came the ice? and the hoary frost of heaven, who hath gendered it? The waters are hid as with a stone, and the face of the deep is frozen." Then he ripped out the page, folded it, placed it in his pocket, and dropped the Bible to the ice. He urged the crew to follow his example. He explained that to survive they needed to travel light. Each man would be allowed to carry with him two pounds of personal gear essential for survival, along with his diary, tobacco, and a spoon and knife. Everything else needed to be discarded, no matter how valuable or sentimental it was.

The men followed Ernest's example. Books, chess sets, playing cards, flags, lanterns, tools, sewing kits, lucky talismans, razors, combs, scissors, extra clothes, even photographs of loved ones piled up. Ernest made one exception, telling Leonard Hussey to bring his banjo. He knew they would all need cheering up along the way.

The *Endurance* had three lifeboats, the *James Caird*, the biggest of the three at 22½ feet long, the *Dudley Docker*, and the *Stancomb Wills*. Ernest decided they would haul the *James Caird* and the *Dudley Docker* with them across the ice and use them to reach Paulet Island. Chippy McNish and Thomas McLeod supervised the loading of the two lifeboats onto sledges while the rest of the crew sorted their equipment. Although the dogs were necessary to help pull the sledges laden with supplies, there were not enough rations to feed all of them. Ernest reluctantly ordered the younger dogs to be put down.

At two o'clock in the afternoon of Saturday, October 30, 1915, the group left the wrecked *Endurance* behind and started across the ice. Ernest, Leonard, James Wordie, and Hubert Hudson rode in the lead sledge as the dogs pulled it. They carried shovels, picks, and axes to chop a path through the jumble of pressure ridges and jagged ice floes. As they made their way forward, the other dog teams followed, each pulling a sledge loaded with nine hundred pounds of stores and equipment. Bringing up the rear came fifteen crewmen man-hauling the two lifeboats on sledge runners. Each boat was loaded with food and equipment and weighed about a ton. The men were harnessed together and would drag one boat a quarter mile before returning and hauling the second boat the quarter mile. Ernest was concerned that the ice might crack beneath the men, leaving them trapped on different ice floes. He kept the group as close together as possible, with the trailing boat never more than a quarter mile away.

Hauling the boats was challenging. The wet snow covering the ice made the boats hard to pull. Sometimes a dog team needed to be unharnessed from its sledge and hitched to the boat to aid the men as they dragged it up and over a pressure ridge in the ice.

After two hours of hauling the boats, the men had covered one mile and were exhausted. Ernest ordered a stop to the trek, and they set up camp for the night. After an improvised meal, they climbed into their tents to sleep.

The following morning they set out again. During the night more wet snow had fallen, making their task even more difficult. As they traveled along, Frank Worsley talked to the Boss. The Skipper was worried that the boats would be damaged and rendered useless as they were dragged over jagged ice ridges. Ernest agreed. He was also wondering about the trek. They seemed to be getting nowhere. After three hours of hauling and covering only another three quarters of a mile, Ernest called a halt. They were on a large, flat ice floe over a half mile in diameter. He decided it was probably the best place they would find to set up a camp. The men pitched their tents on the ice and once again crawled inside them to sleep.

As everyone else slept, Ernest scouted ahead. As far as he could see around them, the ice was an impassable nightmare of pressure ridges, upturned floes, and icebergs. It was impossible for the group to go any farther. He decided they would stay camped where they were and let the drifting ice carry them north to a position where it would be easier to set out for Paulet Island.

After the men awoke, Ernest told them of his decision. The men were relieved. Throughout the next several days, they made a number of trips back to the *Endurance* and Dump Camp, as they'd called the pile of supplies and equipment beside the wrecked ship. They ferried more than three tons of food to their new campsite, which they had named Ocean Camp. They also dragged over the *Stancomb Wills,* the third lifeboat.

As the men ferried food stores, Ernest had Chippy concentrate on salvaging as much useful material as possible from the *Endurance.* Soon Chippy was prying nails from her decking and piling up any useful lumber he could find. He also recovered the timber aboard that was to have been used for a winter hut for the landing party.

Since the new camp was only two miles from the ship, some of the men sought out various personal items from the abandoned pile, particularly their books, with which they could fill in time. And to Frank Hurley's delight, Walter How and William Bakewell made their way below deck and, wading through icy water, retrieved the boxes containing more than four hundred of his glass photographic plates.

The boxes were too heavy to take with them over the ice. But like Frank, Ernest was reluctant to lose the complete photographic record of the expedition so far. He and Frank decided to choose the best 150 photos and take those with them. The rest would have to be left behind. They sat on the ice beside the ship and labored over their decisions. When they had chosen 150 photo plates, Ernest smashed the rest of them. He hated to do it, but he knew that it was the only way to stop Frank from sneaking back and retrieving more of the plates. He also let Frank keep a Kodak 3A camera, along with its leather case and three rolls of film.

To Ernest's surprise, Frank was as good at metalwork as he was at photography. Using the recovered ash chute from the *Endurance*'s boilers and working with limited tools, he made a camp stove. It was designed to burn blubber and could boil three gallons of water from ice in half an hour.

While Frank fashioned the stove, Chippy recovered the ship's wheelhouse and erected it at Ocean Camp as the galley. The stove, which the men called the hot potato can, was installed in the new galley. Then Charles got to work. Soon hot tea and cocoa were available, and stew was simmering in a pot on the stove. Ernest noted that the only problem with the stove, at least for Charles, was the thick, greasy smoke the burning blubber produced. It wasn't unusual for the cook to emerge from the galley coughing and gasping for air, his face a greasy black. But he always had a smile on his face.

Ernest kept a watchful eye on the men. He wished they were all as cheerful as the cook, but many of them were anxious and on edge. Living in close quarters in tents didn't help. If he sensed any tension among the occupants of a tent, Ernest would make a change in tent assignments or quietly take a person aside for a talk. His efforts paid off, and no fights broke out in camp.

On November 12, 1915, the temperature on the ice reached thirty-five degrees Fahrenheit. The men enjoyed the warmer weather and basked in the sun. But the warm temperatures had a downside. The ice beneath their tents and the camp began to melt. And despite using salvaged wood and sealskins in an effort to keep the tent floors dry, the men were wet most of the time. There were many times when a man would take a step and plunge waist deep into a hole made by melted ice.

As he had from the beginning, Frank Worsley charted their position. The ice floe they were camped on was taking them three miles each day farther north and closer to Paulet Island. Ernest knew that if they were carried far enough north, they would reach the edge of the ice and be able to launch the three lifeboats. In preparation, Frank carefully studied the navigational charts he had brought with him from the *Endurance*, eying a possible course for Paulet Island. Ernest asked him to also plot courses for Elephant Island, Clarence Island, even South Georgia, in case they couldn't make it to Paulet Island. Each day the Skipper took sightings of the sun with his sextant and calculated their current location. Sometimes they were headed due north, other days they would deviate a mile or so to the west or east. But whatever the direction, they were inching toward the edge of the pack ice.

Meanwhile, Chippy worked to make the lifeboats more seaworthy. Using wood and nails recovered from the *Endurance*, he raised the gunwales of the *James Caird* fifteen inches and the *Dudley Docker* ten inches. All he had to work with were a saw, a hammer, a chisel, and an adze. He filled in the seams between the added planks to make them watertight, using wool yarn unraveled from a scarf that he caulked over with some of George Marston's oil paints.

"She's going, boys!" Ernest's voice boomed on the night of November 21, 1915. The men scrambled from their tents to find the Boss perched on an ice hill pointing into the distance. As the men looked, a mile and a half away they saw the *Endurance*'s bow slip beneath the water. Moments later the whole ship sank, the ice quickly closing over her. It was a somber moment. The men were completely alone on the ice. There was no going back to salvage anything more from the *Endurance*. The ice had taken her.

As spring gave way to summer, the ice floe under Ocean Camp began breaking apart, and the ice started turning to slush. On December 1, Ernest gave the order to move Ocean Camp to firmer ice about fifty yards away. The men worked hard, and by December 5 the new camp was set up. They celebrated their departure from South Georgia exactly one year before.

As they approached the height of summer, it was light twenty-four hours a day. Yet the men did their best to hold themselves to a night-and-day routine.

During the day some men went off in hunting parties and brought back penguins and seals to eat and to feed the dogs. The dogs were tethered in teams to wires secured to their sledges. The sledges themselves were loaded and the harnesses secured in place ready for the dogs in case they had to move at short notice if the ice under them began breaking up.

During the first three weeks of December, the pack ice continued to move. Unfortunately, it was moving east instead of north, and the easterly drift was taking them away from the Antarctic Peninsula and Paulet Island. This concerned Ernest. If they continued in that direction, they would reach open water with no landfall within easy reach of the boats. Their best hope of survival was to the west. As they continued drifting east, Ernest decided to break camp and move. They would head west over the ice and try to put themselves in a better position to reach one of the islands at the end of the Antarctic Peninsula. Ernest announced that they would celebrate Christmas the following day and on December 23 would pack up camp and leave.

Since they couldn't take all their food stores with them, Ernest allowed the men to eat as much as they wanted for Christmas dinner. And they certainly ate, consuming cans of baked beans, anchovies in oil, canned rabbit, ham, sausages, canned milk, biscuits, coffee, pickles, parsnips, and peaches. It was a grand feast. Ernest had no idea how long it would be before they ate a full meal again.

Chapter 16

Prisoners of the Ice

The following day they were on their way. Once more fifteen men man-hauled the *James Caird* and the *Dudley Docker* over the ice. Ernest decided to leave the *Stancomb Wills* behind, though Frank Worsley disagreed. He argued that when they reached open ocean, the two boats, with the whole crew spread between them, would sit so low and heavy in the water that they would be difficult, perhaps impossible, even for seasoned sailors, to maneuver. Ernest understood the Skipper's concerns, but there was no way they had the manpower to drag three boats that far. It was a risk they would have to take.

As before, they hauled one boat a quarter mile and returned for the second one. Hour after hour they slogged on, often sinking to their knees in melting ice, their boots filling with water. After three days they had struggled forward a total of seven miles.

As the trek continued, the men became discouraged. On December 27, 1915, Ernest noticed that the men who were supposed to be hauling the boats had stopped and were standing around Chippy. He went to see what the problem was and discovered that the fifty-one-year-old carpenter was refusing to take another step. After a lifetime at sea, Chippy knew his maritime law. He told Ernest that the articles he had signed when joining the *Endurance* were no longer valid. Under maritime law, if a ship sank, her crew were free of all obligation to their captain. Their pay ceased and their duties terminated. As a result, he would no longer take orders from Ernest, Frank Worsley, or anyone else. He was not going on.

The situation was serious. Ernest imagined that the other seamen who signed the articles felt the same, though none of them had yet sided with the carpenter. He knew he had to act fast. The only way they would survive was by sticking together. Staying behind, as Chippy was advocating, meant certain death.

Ernest returned to his sledge and brought back a copy of the articles that each man had signed upon joining the *Endurance*'s crew. Since signing the articles was a standard formality when joining a ship, he doubted that any of the men had read those for the *Endurance*. He told Chippy that the articles he had signed were altered slightly. He read the particular articles aloud.

> All members of the Crew without exception to have interchangeable duties. . . . The Crew agree to conduct themselves in an orderly,

> faithful, honest, and sober manner, and to be at all times diligent in their respective Duties, and to be obedient to the lawful commands of the said Master or any Person who shall lawfully succeed him . . . *whether on board, in boats, or on shore* . . . disobedience to lawful commands will be legally punishable.

Ernest explained that he was the Master, and even though they were on pack ice, the crewmen were technically on shore and therefore still legally under his command. The articles had not terminated with the sinking of the *Endurance*. The crew were still on the payroll. In the face of this, Chippy's resistance faded and the men set out again hauling the boats. Although an insurrection was averted, Ernest knew that his crew were nearing the end of their physical and mental limits. Nearly a year had passed since they became trapped in the ice, and no one knew how much longer it would be before they were out of danger.

The men trekked on for another two and a half miles, but the condition of the ice made it increasingly difficult to traverse. Ernest knew that at their present speed the ice drift would sweep them past Paulet Island before they reached open sea, where they could launch the lifeboats. He called a halt to the trek and told the men they would set up camp and wait to see where the ice took them. They named it Patience Camp.

The new camp was nowhere near as comfortable as Ocean Camp. The men missed the scrap wood and sealskins they had used to try to keep their tent floors dry. This new ice floe was in much worse condition than the ice under Ocean Camp had been. It was also smaller and less stable.

Charles soon had a new galley up and running. It consisted of four oars stood upright on the ice and a sheet of canvas wrapped around them to make a shelter. In the middle of the new galley sat the hot potato can to cook on.

New Year's Day 1916 started ominously. A twelve-foot-long leopard seal lunged up onto the ice and chased after Thomas Orde-Lees, who was near the edge of the floe. Thomas let out a yell, and Ernest emerged from his tent to see Frank Wild aim his rifle and shoot the leopard seal. It was a reminder of the dangers lurking on and under the ice. Leopard seals were second only to killer whales as Antarctica's top predators. It was not uncommon to see killer whales break the surface of pools of water amid the ice. Ernest knew that they needed to be vigilant. At this time of year, as the ice thinned, killer whales were known to swim below, searching for the shadows of seals basking on the ice above. They would then lunge up through the ice, jaws open, and snatch the unsuspecting seal to eat. Ernest was concerned that a killer whale might mistake one of the men for a seal and attack from below through the ice.

On Thursday, January 13, Ernest decided that most of the dogs had to be killed. It required a seal a day to feed them, and while seals had been around when the men first arrived at Patience Camp, their numbers were dwindling. Besides, the men couldn't take the dogs with them in the boats. It seemed to

Ernest a waste of resources to keep feeding them when one seal would feed all the men for several days. In the end, three dog teams were kept alive. They would be used for some of the men to return to Ocean Camp and haul back more supplies.

Two days later, seventy-mile-per-hour winds began lashing the ice floe. The gale kept up for six days, making life at Patience Camp even more miserable. According to Frank Worsley's calculations, the wind was driving their ice floe rapidly north. On January 21, 1916, Frank announced that they had crossed the Antarctic Circle. Ernest was happy with the northerly progress. To celebrate he issued each man an extra round of hot Virol, a powdered nutritional drink mix.

Once again Frank Worsley voiced concern to Ernest about the boats. He pointed out that the gale that had blown their ice floe speedily north had also blown the ice floe on which Ocean Camp was located closer to them. He requested that some men be allowed to return to the old camp and haul back the *Stancomb Wills.* Ernest wasn't sure that that was a good idea. It meant that a number of men would be away from Patience Camp and might permanently be separated if conditions suddenly changed. Still, he promised to consider the idea. Each day the Skipper pestered him about the boat. At the end of January, Ernest relented and allowed Frank Wild to select eighteen men to go and retrieve the *Stancomb Wills.*

The trip was a success, and no one was more relieved than Ernest when they all returned safely hauling the *Stancomb Wills.* Now the Skipper had his extra boat. Several men returned again to Ocean Camp with sledges and dog teams and hauled back the remaining supplies from there. When this had been done, two more dog teams were killed, leaving just one team.

At their exposed camp, the conditions took a toll on the men physically. The wind made their eyes water. The dripping tears formed small icicles on their noses and cheeks that would break off and tear away small patches of skin. And their meat-heavy diet caused them to become constipated and flatulent. They were also filthy. Grease and grime were imbedded in their hands and faces and smudged all over their outer clothing, which was wearing thin. At the end of each day Charles was totally covered in sooty black grease from cooking over the hot potato can. Ernest made sure that he received the last bar of soap.

The situation was dire. Ernest stayed calm during the day to reassure the men, but at night he had many nightmares about what could go wrong. When he awoke, he would take each nightmare as a warning and would work out a plan of what he could do should that particular scenario occur.

As with the men, waiting was the hardest thing for Ernest. In his diary on February 1, 1916, he wrote, "No news. S.E. wind, fine weather. Patience, Patience, Patience."

The monotony was broken on Sunday, February 20, when Ernest and the rest of the crew crawled from their tents to discover that a huge flock of migrating Adélie penguins had invaded their ice floe.

The blubber supply for the stove was running low, and the men sprang into action, capturing and killing as many penguins as possible. By the time the Adélies moved on two days later, the men had a good supply of blubber to fuel the stove and meat to eat.

As the days passed, the men read and reread the books they had brought with them. They also talked exhaustively about every subject imaginable. Sometimes they exercised by walking around and around the ice floe. But mostly they waited.

More than a year had passed since the *Endurance* had become stuck in the ice, and now all Ernest could do was wait like the men, always eager to hear Frank Worsley's latest report of their position and paying attention for any sign that they might be nearing the edge of the ice pack. That sign came on Thursday, March 9, when Ernest felt the swell of the ocean slowly lift their ice floe. The men felt it too and watched as the ice around them rose and fell to the rhythm of the swell beneath. They were close to the open sea.

Now the men had something new to talk about. Ernest could feel their hope rising, but it didn't last. Slowly the pack ice closed in harder around their floe until they could no longer feel the movement of the ocean below. At the same time the weather began to deteriorate. The Antarctic winter wasn't far away. The temperatures dropped below zero at night, adding to everyone's misery. Now, in the morning, each man lashed up and stowed his gear, ready for a fast escape in the boats if the ice below them suddenly broke up. They also had to move the boats from one place to another, lest the sledge runners they sat on freeze in place, making it impossible to launch the boats.

In the middle of March, Frank informed Ernest that they had drifted too far north to reach Paulet Island in the boats. To get there they would have to beat against the fierce wind of the Southern Ocean, and the boats would never make it. The Danger Islands to the east of Paulet Island became Ernest's new destination. These islands were visible on the horizon, but their ice floe drifted past them as Ernest watched in despair. Ernest then turned his attention to Clarence Island and Elephant Island, the two easternmost islands of the South Shetland group. Since no one had ever landed on these islands, Ernest had no idea what they might find there. All he knew was that they were the last two islands to which they could possibly escape when they took to the boats.

On the ice floe the men filled the time repairing their clothing and equipment in preparation for the next stage of their journey. As the ice continued to deteriorate, Ernest ordered two men at a time to be constantly looking for cracks. Their lives depended on moving quickly if the ice broke up.

The blubber supply for the stove began running low again. Ernest limited hot food to once a day, with the other meals served cold. He hated doing it, especially since the temperature was dropping, but he had little choice.

Now that they were above the Antarctic Circle, for the first time since entering the ice on the *Endurance*, the men endured another misery—rain. Soon their sleeping bags and blankets, along with everything else in camp, were sodden. Some of the men began doubting they would ever leave the ice. They felt doomed to die its prisoners. Aware of the deteriorating physical and mental condition of the men, Ernest did his best to encourage them. He went from tent to tent asking how everyone was getting on and engaging the men in long conversations about any topic that would distract them.

Ernest's mind constantly churned with escape plans. He knew that whalers and other explorers never stopped at either Clarence or Elephant Island. Both islands were nothing more than rocky outcrops. Whatever island the group made it to, someone would have to set out from there to bring help back to the others. Ernest, Frank Wild, and the Skipper talked among themselves about how they might do it.

"Crack! Crack! Quickly, lash up and stow! Lash up and stow!" Alf Cheetham, the watchman, yelled in the early hours of March 28. Ernest leapt from his tent to see two cracks running across their ice floe. He joined the men as they followed their emergency drill, quickly breaking down the camp, stowing tents, sleeping bags, and other equipment. Several men freed the sledge runners of the boats from the ice. Then as they made sure they were all on the same piece of ice and waited, another crack opened up beneath the *James Caird*, which was quickly pulled to safety.

Once it appeared that the ice would not break beneath them anymore, the men relaxed and stood around eating a cold breakfast. As they ate, a large leopard seal lunged up onto their ice floe. Immediately Frank Wild sprang into action, killing the seal with one rifle bullet. As several men cut up the leopard seal, they discovered fifty undigested fish inside its stomach, a wonderful find. One moment they had been eating a cold breakfast because of a shortage of blubber and rations. Now they had plenty of fish, a thousand pounds of seal meat, and enough blubber to keep the stove fired. Ernest decided they would have a feast and eat the seal's liver for lunch.

After the feast, Ernest ordered the last team of dogs killed. It was obvious the ice pack was breaking up around them. The dogs were no longer of use and would have no place on the boats. Their meat was butchered for the men to eat.

Since their ice floe was deteriorating, Ernest ordered all the men to alternate four hours on watch and four hours off. They were to sleep fully clothed with their boots, mittens, and hats on, ready to move at a moment's notice. By now the ice floe was once again rising and falling on the ocean swell. Terns and Cape pigeons flew overhead, all signs that they were approaching open water. Any day now they would be taking to the boats.

By April 3 their ice floe had been whittled down to just two hundred yards across and was surrounded by open leads of water. It bobbed up and down and bumped against other floes, filling the air with the sound of grinding and creaking. Killer whales breached the surface in the leads, blowing spray that quickly turned to ice crystals in the bitter cold.

Although open water surrounded them, Ernest still thought it too dangerous to launch the boats. The ice floes were still crashing into each other and could easily crush the boats if they got caught between them. They would have to wait a little longer before putting to sea.

By Saturday, April 8, 1916, the ice floe was just fifty yards across and continuing to crack and break apart. It was time to leave Patience Camp. After taking a sextant reading of the sun and fixing their position, Frank Worsley informed the Boss that they had drifted over six hundred miles since the *Endurance* first became trapped in the ice. It was now time for the twenty-eight men to take their chances in three small boats against the Southern Ocean and try to make it to Clarence or Elephant Island.

Chapter 17

Back on Solid Ground

At 12:40 in the early afternoon the boats left Patience Camp. Ernest and Frank Wild led the way in the *James Caird*, with ten other men aboard. The *Dudley Docker* followed with Frank Worsley and another eight men. The *Stancomb Wills* brought up the rear with Tom Crean, Hubert Hudson, and the remaining five men. The men rowed slowly and carefully amid the ice toward the northwest. Rowing wasn't easy, especially in the *James Caird* and the *Dudley Docker*, whose gunwales had been raised. To get the oars at the correct angle to the water, the rowers had to sit on boxes of stores atop the thwarts. Throughout the afternoon the men took turns at the oars. They picked their way along leads of water. As the light began to fade in the late afternoon, Ernest spotted an ice floe big enough to camp on overnight.

The boats pulled up to the ice floe and were unloaded, and camp was set up. The crabeater seal that basked on the floe when they arrived was quickly shot and was soon being prepared for dinner. After eating, the men lay down to sleep.

"Someone's missing," came a cry in the middle of the night. Jolted awake, Ernest looked to see an object in the water. He leapt up, raced over, grabbed the object, and heaved it onto the ice. The object turned out to be a sleeping bag with Ernest Holness inside. Moments later, the newly split ice floe crashed back together. It then drifted apart again, with men on both sections. Frank Worsley threw a rope. Ernest grabbed the other end. Together with several other men they hauled the two chunks of ice back together.

"We must get everything onto a single floe before the ice splits again!" Ernest yelled. "And two men need to walk Holness to warm him so he doesn't freeze to death. We don't have any dry clothes to put him in, so keep him moving."

Men sprang into action, working furiously to get the lifeboats and all of the equipment and stores onto a single piece of ice. Ernest Holness was marched back and forth. Already his outer clothes were frozen, and they crackled as he walked.

Once everything and everyone were on the same piece of ice, there was no more sleeping. The men gathered around the hot potato can for warmth. Every two hours Charles cooked more steaks from the crabeater seal. Shortly after five o'clock, dawn broke. It was misty and overcast, and as soon as it was light enough, Ernest had the boats launched, and the men climbed aboard.

The three boats continued heading northwest following open leads of water. By late morning they broke free of the ice. They had finally reached open sea. Ernest gave the order to stow the oars and hoist the sails. Spray washed across the boats, dousing the men. The water instantly turned to ice, freezing the men's clothes. Ernest wrapped his arms around himself and tried to stay warm, an impossible task.

Rounding a large ice floe, Ernest hoped they would have a straight run to Clarence or Elephant Island. However, the ice floe had been protecting them from the full force of the Southern Ocean. Once they had sailed around it, the sea was so rough that the boats could not make any headway. There was no escaping the fact that the vessels were too heavily laden for the ocean conditions. Besides carrying the twenty-eight men, the boats held three tents, spare clothing, sleeping bags, blankets, Primus stoves and paraffin fuel, cooking utensils, the hot potato can, sledging rations, three weeks' supply of food, and Frank Hurley's metal box of glass photographic plates, along with the oars, masts, sails, and ropes. They had no choice but to return to the shelter of the ice and lighten the load.

Ernest led them to an iceberg worn down by the sea. Its large, flat surface rose about twenty feet above the water, with a place on one side about five feet up, where they landed the boats and pulled them to safety. To lighten the boats, Ernest decided a week's worth of food needed to be discarded. Charles cooked a hearty meal for them all using the extra supplies. After the meal, the men crawled into their sleeping bags or wrapped themselves in their wool blankets. They hadn't slept properly in thirty-six hours.

The following morning, Tuesday, April 11, Ernest awoke to a discouraging sight. As far as he could see, the loose pack ice had closed in around them, and thirty-foot ocean swells were causing the ice to rise and fall. As their iceberg rode the swell, it was being chipped away at the edges by constant collisions with the ice floes. Worse, there were no open leads in which to launch the boats. They were stuck on an iceberg that Ernest feared would capsize, taking them with it.

Ernest, Frank Wild, and Frank Worsley climbed to the highest point on the iceberg to keep a lookout for open water. It wasn't until two in the afternoon that they spotted an open lead. By then the iceberg had been worn away to the size of a tennis court. Ernest gave the order to launch the boats. Soon they were on their way again, rowing down the lead to open ocean.

Once clear of the ice, the boats' sails were hoisted. The *James Caird* and the *Dudley Docker* sped along with the wind, but the *Stancomb Wills*, the smallest of the boats and the only one without her gunwales extended, was slow. Ernest ordered the *Dudley Docker* to go back and take the *Stancomb Wills* in tow.

As night fell, Ernest didn't want to risk camping on the ice. Instead, he had the boats head for shelter beside a large ice floe. After mooring alongside, Charles climbed onto the floe, where he set up the stove and boiled water so they could enjoy a hot drink. After the drink, the wind changed and began blowing jagged ice chunks toward them. Quickly the cook and stove were loaded aboard, and Ernest gave the order to start rowing away from the ice.

Once the men reached safety, Ernest had the three boats tied together so they wouldn't be separated in the dark. Throughout the night the men took turns rowing as the temperature dropped to zero degrees Fahrenheit. The men were grateful when dawn brought a change in wind direction and the temperature rose to about thirty degrees.

The wind change also opened up the clouds. For the first time in days, Frank Worsley was able to get a sighting on the sun with his sextant and chart their position. Ernest had the *James Caird* come about and maneuver alongside the *Dudley Docker* to find out what it was. "How much distance have we made, Skipper?" he asked.

Frank pulled himself close to Ernest and whispered into his ear. "Thirty miles astern, Sir."

Ernest was shocked but tried not to show it. All the while, he had thought they were making good progress to the northwest. Instead, the current had been driving them backward! He decided not to tell the men how far they had fallen behind. It would be too discouraging. "Not as much westing as we'd hoped for, boys! Sail on," he said.

That night the boats again sheltered beside a large ice floe, and once more the wind changed, driving jagged ice chunks close to them. In a repeat of the previous evening, Ernest gave the order to man the oars, and they spent the rest of the night picking their way through the ice and back to open water.

At dawn, Ernest was shocked to see the condition of his crew. Their faces were pale with black rings under their eyes, and their beards and hair were caked white with frozen sea spray. He needed to get the men safely away from the ice as quickly as possible. Frank Worsley estimated that Elephant Island lay one hundred miles to their north, and Ernest decided that that was the island to head for. The island was only twenty miles long, and Ernest hoped that the Skipper's reckoning was right. If they missed Elephant Island, beyond lay six hundred miles of the roughest ocean on earth. There was no way they or their boats would survive an attempt to cross it to the tip of South America.

The sails were hoisted, and once again the *James Caird* led the way. The wind pushed them northward well beyond the pack ice and far out into the open sea. Large waves broke across the bows of the boats, and spray drenched the men. Again the *Stancomb Wills* struggled in the surging ocean. Ernest feared that the boat might be lost and ordered it tethered to the *James Caird.*

The three boats sailed on together. As night descended, Ernest ordered them to be tied up together again and for the *Dudley Docker* to put out a sea anchor. This was a cone-shaped piece of canvas attached to the boat by a line. The drag the anchor created kept the boats headed into the wind so they wouldn't turn broadside to the waves and be swamped.

With darkness, the temperature again dropped rapidly, but not the wind, which buffeted the boats. Icy water lay in the bottom of the *James Caird*, and Ernest's boots and feet were wet. Ernest wiggled his toes vigorously to keep the blood flowing and stave off frostbite. He advised the men to do likewise. Some of them were already suffering frostbite, and many had saltwater boils on their faces. Whenever a man moved in one of the boats, his frozen outer clothes would crackle. As the night wore on, Ernest could hear the muffled sounds of men crying. Despite their agony, all the men, including Ernest, took turns chipping ice off the bows and thwarts of the boats. If they didn't, the heavy ice would drag the vessels down so low in the water they would sink.

At daybreak Ernest surveyed the men. They had all survived the night, but they were in grim physical shape. He could feel his own strength beginning to ebb under the brutal conditions. By now another problem had presented itself—thirst. In fleeing the pack ice to avoid the boats being crushed, there hadn't been time to load ice aboard to melt for drinking water. The salt water, absorbed through everyone's skin, was making the men urinate frequently. A number of the men had diarrhea from the uncooked seal meat they had been eating since taking to the boats. The salt water and diarrhea combined to make the men extremely thirsty. Ernest wondered if it might drive some of them mad.

All Ernest could do to lift his men's spirits was point their gaze to the snow-covered peaks rising above the horizon not more than thirty miles away—Elephant

Island. The sea anchor was hauled in, and the *Dudley Docker* was untied from the other two boats. If all went well, they would be standing on land by nightfall.

With sails hoisted, the boats were off again. This time the *Dudley Docker* took the lead while the *James Caird* continued towing the *Stancomb Wills*. The wind pushed the boats forward at a steady clip, though Ernest knew it wasn't fast enough for the men. As they sailed along, some men chewed raw seal meat, allowing the blood to ease their parched, swelling throats.

By midafternoon they were ten miles from Elephant Island when a strong current stalled progress. Then the wind shifted, forcing them to quickly lower the sail lest they be blown backward. The exhausted men tried to muster their strength and row the rest of the way, but the current was too strong. Ernest could scarcely believe it. They were so close to land, yet they would have to spend another grueling night at sea in the boats. Ernest fretted that some of the men might not survive.

After darkness fell, the wind reached gale force. Ernest allowed the *Dudley Docker* to separate from the other two boats. It was now too dangerous for them to be so close. Throughout the night the *James Caird* and the *Stancomb Wills* drifted together in the churning ocean. All night Ernest sat at the rear of the boat, his hand firmly on the painter line securing the *Stancomb Wills* to the *James Caird*, making sure the smaller boat did not break loose. He also regularly called back to the *Stancomb Wills* to make sure that everyone was all right.

At daybreak, Ernest was relieved to discover that all the men were still alive, though some were delirious. As he scanned the sea around them, he could see no sign of the *Dudley Docker.* Ernest had faith in the Skipper's navigational and sailing skills and was confident that the boat was still afloat somewhere out there.

The wind and the current were now favorable. The sails were hoisted, and the boats headed for Elephant Island. It wasn't long before the two boats were close to shore scouting out a good landing place. By nine thirty in the morning they were waiting off a narrow beach at the base of a cliff. Ernest studied the breakers crashing onto the reef that separated them from the beach. He could see a small break in the reef, through which he thought the boats could squeeze. It was their best hope. Just as he was about to give the order for the men to begin rowing to catch an inbound wave, he spotted the *Dudley Docker* rounding a point and heading toward them.

The men pulled at the oars. Moments later the bottom of the *James Caird* scraped against the gravelly shore, and a shout went up from the men.

"Jump ashore, Blackborow!" Ernest called. He wanted to give the expedition's youngest crew member the honor of being the first man to ever land on Elephant Island.

When Perce failed to move, Ernest reached across and hauled him over the side. But Perce just collapsed onto his hands and knees in the water.

"Get up," Ernest urged.

"I can't, Sir," he replied. "It's my feet."

In that moment Ernest was mortified by what he had done. He recalled that one of the doctors had told him that Perce's feet had frozen and that several of his toes were severely frostbitten. Quickly Ernest ordered Walter How and William Bakewell to assist Perce ashore. As they did so, the *Dudley Docker* pulled up on the beach beside the other two boats. The men clambered out and struggled ashore. It was Saturday, April 15, 1916, and it was the first time any of them had set foot on land since setting sail from South Georgia sixteen months before.

Ernest was elated. He had gotten his men back on solid ground. He watched as some of them wept while others fell to their knees and picked up handfuls of black pebbles, letting them run through their fingers. Some men ran for the streams of freshwater trickling down the cliff face behind them.

Elephant Island was named for the elephant seals crowded together along its rocky shore. Frank Wild shot one of the seals, and Charles soon had seal steaks sizzling on the hot potato can, which he had set up on the beach.

While he waited for the seal to cook, Ernest studied their surroundings. As he looked up at the cliff face behind the beach, his heart dropped.

Chapter 18

Beating the Odds

The cliffs behind the beach loomed straight up eight hundred feet, but it was the high-water mark several feet up the cliff face that caught Ernest's attention. Sometimes, probably during storms at high tide, the entire beach was underwater. He knew they couldn't stay there for long. The beach was a death trap.

Ernest decided not to say anything about it right away. The men needed food and rest before they learned that they would all have to take to the boats again. Like the rest of the men, Ernest hungrily devoured the cooked seal steaks. Then, too exhausted to pitch tents, the men all lay down on the beach and slept.

Ernest was up early the next morning, but he let the rest of the crew sleep until nine thirty. Frank Wild was up too, and he shot several more seals to eat and keep the stove fueled. Once everyone was awake, Ernest pointed to the high-water mark on the cliff face and broke the news that they needed to take to the boats once more in search of a better landing spot. Shortly before midday, Frank Wild and five other men pushed the *Stancomb Wills* into the water and rowed out to sea to scout for another location.

Darkness had fallen when they returned. Much to Ernest's relief, Frank reported finding a suitable spot seven miles along the coast to the west. It was a narrow spit of land with a glacier on the mountainside to supply drinking water, and a penguin rookery at one end for food. He assured Ernest that the beach sloped steeply up with enough dry land above the high-water mark on which to camp.

Ernest had everyone up at five the following morning loading stores and equipment back into the boats. The boats were launched and the men climbed in. They began rowing westward along the rocky coast. Once more the weather was a challenge. A fierce wind blew up, drenching the men with freezing sea spray and sapping their meager energy as they rowed forward. But they kept at it and by midafternoon were hauling the boats up onto the spit Frank had recommended.

Ernest looked over the new campsite. The spit was bare and windswept, but the back of the beach was elevated enough so their camp wouldn't be swept away in a storm. However, the beach was so exposed that the wind ripped the first tent to shreds when the men tried to erect it. Not wanting any more tents destroyed, Ernest had the men sleep on the beach in the open. But the storm that had buffeted them on the way along the coast intensified into a howling blizzard. For two days Ernest and the men huddled in reindeer-skin sleeping bags or wrapped themselves in wool blankets as snow piled up against their backs.

When the storm cleared, the men killed penguins at the rookery at the end of the spit. The birds were soon cooked, their blubber fueling the fire that cooked them.

Although the men were now on safe, solid ground and wouldn't be washed away in a storm, Ernest knew that they couldn't hold on for long on Elephant Island. They were freezing and malnourished, and some were on the verge of madness. There was no chance that a whaling boat would find them there. If they were to be rescued, someone needed to go for help. This was something Ernest had thought about ever since it seemed they would be landing on either Clarence or Elephant Island. Cape Horn at the tip of South America was the nearest inhabited land and six hundred miles north. But at this time of year, the wind and the ocean swell were against them. To set out in the boats for Cape Horn would be certain death. Ernest had another plan. Taking advantage of the direction of the wind and current, he and several men would set out in a single boat for South Georgia, eight hundred miles to the northeast. At one of the whaling stations there, they could raise the alarm and bring a ship back to get the rest of the men.

Ernest knew that the plan was risky. He would be crossing the roughest, most dangerous ocean in the world, and he planned to do it in the *James Caird*, a 22½-foot-long open boat. This had never been done before, and the odds were against their success. Yet it was the only hope Ernest could see for the survival of his men. He had talked it over with Frank Worsley before leaving the pack ice. And while the Skipper thought it foolhardy, he agreed that such a voyage might be possible.

Ernest told Frank Wild his plan. Frank immediately volunteered to go in the boat. As much as Ernest would have liked him at his side in the boat, he knew that he needed Frank's leadership skills on Elephant Island to help ensure the survival of those left behind until they were rescued. Instead, he chose Frank Worsley and four others—Tom Crean, Tim McCarthy, Chippy McNish, and John Vincent—to go with him. Ernest gave them four days to prepare for the journey.

Having chosen a crew and a departure date, Ernest announced the plan to the rest of the men. Despite the weather conditions, the whole camp sprang into action making preparations. Chippy prepared the *James Caird* for the voyage. He strengthened the gunwales and, using sledge runners, Venesta plywood from the packing crates, and canvas, enclosed much of the boat with a deck, leaving a rectangle cockpit open at the back for the helmsman. The *Dudley Docker*'s mast was used to strengthen the *James Caird*'s keel, while the *Stancomb Wills*'s mast and sail were fitted as a mizzen at the rear of the cockpit. Bags were stitched together from old blankets and filled with fifteen hundred pounds of rocks for ballast to stop the boat from capsizing while under sail in the rough sea.

Once the strengthening and modifications were made to the *James Caird*, attention was turned to equipping and provisioning the boat. Glacial ice was melted to fill two kegs with drinking water for the trip. Bouillon cubes, sugar, powdered milk, biscuits, and six weeks' worth of sledging rations for the men were loaded aboard. A Primus stove and fuel, a pot, spoons, and six small bowls were also loaded into the boat, along with six reindeer sleeping bags and a hand pump for bailing. Lastly, Frank Worsley's navigational equipment—a compass, his sextant, navigation tables, charts, a pencil, a notebook, and a chronometer—were stowed aboard.

Early on Monday morning, April 24, 1916, the *James Caird* and her six crew members set out from Elephant Island. "Good luck to you, Boss!" yelled the twenty-two men left behind. Ernest waved at them one last time and then set his attention on the boat.

Ernest and Frank agreed that they should sail as far north as possible before turning eastward toward South Georgia. It wasn't long before Ernest watched Elephant Island slip below the horizon behind them. When darkness fell, they continued sailing full speed ahead.

Ernest divided the men into two groups, with Tom, Chippy, and himself in one, and Frank, John, and Tim in the other. While one group manned the boat, the other would sleep below the deck in the bow, where the sleeping bags were laid out. After four hours they would trade places.

At the end of his first watch, Ernest discovered just how cramped and uncomfortable it was going to be on the boat. He crawled on hands and knees over the ballast rocks and then wriggled on his stomach across the crates containing their stores to the space in the bow. He had barely enough room to maneuver into his sleeping bag, and it wasn't easy to get to sleep as the *James Caird*'s bow constantly lifted and fell as it cut through the waves.

Cooking below deck was also a challenge. Tom was cook for the voyage, but since the boat pitched and rolled so much, Frank helped out. From his position at the tiller in the cockpit, Ernest watched Tom and Frank as they sat opposite each other, balancing the Primus stove upright with their feet. Frank held the pot while Tom mixed the chunks of pemmican with water and waited for it to boil. Whenever the boat pitched or rolled, Frank lifted the pot off the stove so it wouldn't spill. He would then place it down again when the boat stabilized so that Tom could continue mixing the hoosh.

Three days out from Elephant Island the weather deteriorated into a gale. Snow fell, and the ocean swell increased. Waves crashed across the *James Caird*, and water streamed into the boat. The men on watch were kept busy bailing water. Everything below deck was wet, including the reindeer sleeping bags that began to rot and stink. Reindeer hair began separating from the skin and got into everything: their food, their nostrils, and their mouths.

Despite the discomfort, the men sailed on. The boat would ride up the face of the huge waves rolling across the Southern Ocean. It would be battered by the wind before sliding down into the relative calm of the trough between waves before rising again on the next wave. All the while, the person manning the helm wrestled with the tiller to keep the *James Caird* on course.

The course was always on Ernest's mind. Beyond South Georgia lay three thousand miles of empty ocean. If they missed the island, they would have nowhere else to land, and the prevailing wind would not allow them to backtrack. Ernest was constantly talking to Frank about where they were. On the third day out, Frank had managed to capture a reading of the sun and determined that they had traveled 128 miles from Elephant Island. But they hadn't seen the sun now in several days to get another reading and fix their position. Yet according to the Skipper's dead reckoning, they were still on course despite the gales and pounding waves. That was good enough for Ernest, who, throughout the ordeal, trusted Frank completely. Frank had a sixth sense for navigating.

On the seventh day of the voyage another gale blew in. The temperature dropped so rapidly that Ernest worried that the sails might become caked in ice and cause the *James Caird* to be top-heavy and capsize. He ordered the sails taken down and stowed below. Then he and Frank set a sea anchor to keep the boat facing into the storm.

The next morning, Ernest could tell that the motion of the boat felt heavy. He soon discovered that she was encased in fifteen inches of ice above the waterline. The men had to act fast or they were in danger of capsizing, even with the sails down. The ice had to be removed. One by one each man took his turn crawling on hands and knees over the icy deck and chipping away the ice with an ax. The bone-chilling work was perilous as waves continued washing across the boat. Every five minutes Ernest had another man replace the one chipping the ice. For that day and most of the next, the men had to crawl out and chip away ice.

When the storm abated, the men were in bad shape: frostbitten, hungry, and covered with painful saltwater blisters. Their legs had been rubbed raw from the constant chafing of their wet trousers. Below deck everything was saturated, and as water was pumped out of the *James Caird*, Ernest took the two most rotted, stinking sleeping bags and threw them overboard.

The sails were once again hoisted and the boat sailed on. But that night the men had to act fast once more to save their vessel. Ernest was at the tiller when a towering rogue wave washed across them from behind, swamping the boat. They sprang into action pumping and bailing with anything they could find, even their hands, to get the water out. It took hours, but they managed to empty out the water and save their boat.

The following day, their tenth at sea, the clouds parted to reveal the sun. Frank grabbed his sextant. He knelt on the thwart in the cockpit, with John and Tim holding tightly around his waist to keep him from being thrown overboard. Meanwhile Ernest squatted in the cockpit, holding the chronometer.

Frank waited until the *James Caird* reached the top of a wave and the horizon was in sight. He then shouted "Now!" as he snapped a reading on the sun's angle above the horizon and Ernest noted the time. With his pencil Frank began doing calculations in a notebook, carefully peeling apart the damp pages of his navigational tables and jotting down the numbers he needed from them. When he was done, he announced they were 444 miles from Elephant Island. They were on course and more than halfway there.

Over the next three days they enjoyed fairer weather, but the sun was visible only once more during that time for Frank to chart their position. They adjusted their course more to the east and sailed on.

About this time they discovered that salt water had seeped into one of the freshwater casks, turning the water brackish. Ernest had no option but to cut their water ration to a half cup a day.

On the evening of their fourteenth day at sea, Ernest saw something that lifted his spirits—a piece of kelp floating in the water. This was a sign that they were nearing land. According to Frank's latest calculation, they were now about eighty miles from South Georgia, approaching from the southwest.

Ernest and the Skipper began talking about where to land. The southwest coastline of the island was uninhabited. The whaling stations were located on the northern coast. They wondered whether to head for the northern coast or take their chances on the southwest side. In the end they decided on the southwest. Heading for the northern coast was too great a risk. If they were swept past the island, they would have no other landfall until Africa.

The morning of their fifteenth day at sea was foggy. At midday the fog lifted, and rain squalls rolled across the ocean. The men were huddled below deck to keep warm when at the helm Tim yelled, "Land ho!" Ernest maneuvered himself into the cockpit, and there, ten miles ahead, lay a snow-covered mountain. "We've done it!" he exclaimed, a broad grin across his face. They had beaten the odds.

As the *James Caird* sailed on, more of the island became visible, and the men could see patches of green tussock grass. Ernest was eager to make landfall as soon as possible, but as had happened so often before on their ordeal across ice and ocean, the weather would not cooperate. A storm descended on them. They would have to wait another night in the boat before landing.

By noon the next day hurricane-force winds accompanied by hail and sleet began lashing them. Worse yet, the wind and waves were pushing them closer to the island's rocky coast. Their only hope of avoiding the *James Caird* being smashed on the rocks was to sail farther out to sea. Ernest knew that this was risky. The boat could easily be swamped or capsize, but there was nothing else they could do.

It took the men an hour to rig the two smallest sails in the howling wind, but once the sails were set, Ernest watched anxiously as Frank took the helm and began making headway, easing the *James Caird* through the waves and away from the rocks. The rest of the men bailed and pumped as water washed across the boat. All afternoon and into the night they worked feverishly to save themselves and their boat from doom.

A little after nine in the evening the storm began to subside. At last the exhausted men could rest, though it was an uncomfortable night. It was still too rough to cook hoosh, and their throats were parched. All of the fresh drinking water was gone.

In the morning as the sun rose, Ernest looked out at the rugged coast of South Georgia. He knew that they must land today. With no water, the men could not hold out much longer. Already he was worried about Chippy, who was in terrible physical shape. Ernest wondered whether he might die before they reached land.

Frank determined that they were nine miles off King Haakon Bay. All the men except Chippy took turns pulling at the boat's two oars. The backbreaking work took all day, but at last they came close enough to see a cove at the entrance to King Haakon Bay where they might be able to land.

Ernest gave the order to head for the cove, and the men redoubled their effort at the oars. Waves crashed over boulders at the cove's mouth, and Ernest stood at the bow directing the boat around them. Then he saw a rocky beach where they could land and had them head for it. Moments later Ernest felt the *James Caird*'s keel scrape on the rocks. The men clambered from the boat and went ashore. It was May 10, 1916. On the seventeenth day after setting out from Elephant Island they had managed to find their way back to South Georgia, the place they had set out from seventeen months before on their way to Antarctica. The men, including Ernest, got down on their hands and knees and lapped freshwater from the stream running down to the ocean.

Chapter 19

Across the Unknown

For two days the men mostly slept, sheltered in a cave that Tom discovered. They huddled for warmth atop damp, rotting sleeping bags, around a fire fueled with old wooden hatch covers, spars, masts, and lockers. They found these on the other side of the cove in a pile of flotsam from wrecked ships washed up over the years. Pitching the pieces of flotsam into the fire reminded Ernest of the unforgiving power of the ocean they had just crossed. Much bigger, better-equipped vessels than the *James Caird* had met their doom in the mountainous swells of the Southern Ocean.

After resting, it was time for action. The whaling stations were still 130 miles away by boat, on the north coast of South Georgia. As Ernest and Frank once more talked about how to get there, they decided not to attempt it in the boat. The risk of being swept out into the Atlantic Ocean was too great. Besides, they weren't sure that the *James Caird* was up to the task. Her hull had been rubbed so thin in places that Ernest feared she might spring a leak and sink if they set out into the rough sea again.

On studying a map of the island, Frank estimated that it was about twenty-two miles directly overland across the island from their position at King Haakon Bay to Stromness Bay, where three whaling stations were located. The trouble was, no one had ever crossed the island's rugged interior. The point was reinforced by Frank's damp map of South Georgia. The map marked the coastline and the names of the bays, but the interior was blank. Yet Ernest knew that the only way to save the men back on Elephant Island was to cross South Georgia on foot to one of the whaling stations. He chose Frank and Tom to accompany him across the island.

The cove the men had landed in was surrounded by cliffs, and the only way out of it was by boat. Four days after arriving, they all packed up and climbed back into the *James Caird.* They were headed to the far end of King Haakon Bay. From there they could climb up to the glacier and into the interior of the island.

After setting up camp at the new location, the men got to work preparing for the overland journey. Ernest decided they should take just the essentials for survival: three days' worth of sledging rations, a small pot, the Primus stove and fuel, biscuits, the carpenter's adze, ninety feet of rope, and Frank's compass and watch. Since they intended to travel as fast as possible, stopping only for short rests, there seemed little point in taking sleeping bags.

At two o'clock in the morning on Thursday, May 18, 1916, the three men set off to cross South Georgia. Tim would stay at King Haakon Bay and watch over John and Chippy, who were both weak from the boat journey. To make their stay more comfortable while they awaited rescue, the *James Caird* was turned upside down, with one side propped up to provide shelter.

Carrying a makeshift knapsack containing their gear, Ernest, Frank, and Tom climbed toward the interior of the island through slushy, ankle-deep snow. Once on the glacier, Frank took out his compass and map, located their position, and pointed in the direction they needed to go to reach Stromness Bay. They roped themselves together and set off. Deep crevasses crisscrossed the glacier. Ernest led the way, stopping every fifteen minutes for a two-minute rest, since all three of them were still weak and tired from the ordeal in the boat.

The men made their way along the glacier, and when dawn broke, they got a clearer look at where they were headed. In front of them stood a row of jagged peaks they had to cross. Between the peaks were four saddles. Ernest stopped to size up the situation and then led on as they began climbing the steep slope to the first saddle, snow crunching beneath their boots.

By late morning they reached the saddle, and even though it was bone-chillingly cold, Ernest was sweating and breathing heavily. He eased up to the edge of the saddle and peered over. He sighted a sheer drop down the other side that they could not pass. The three of them turned and headed down before crossing the face of the mountain to begin ascending to the next pass.

They stopped to cook some hoosh before continuing to climb. Again there was a sheer drop down the other side, and again they trudged back down and over and began climbing to the third pass. Ernest could hardly believe it when they approached another sheer drop down the other side of the mountain. Disheartened and fatigued, they backtracked once more and began climbing to the fourth saddle. Darkness was falling when they reached it. This time there wasn't a sheer drop but a steep ice bank on the other side. "We'll try it. We have no choice," Ernest said, leading the way and cutting steps in the ice with the adze as he went. The other two followed in his footsteps.

The men descended about two hundred yards until Ernest felt the angle of the bank become less steep and become a snowy slope descending into the darkness below. He waited for the others to catch up. Together they peered down the mountain. No one could see where the slope ended. With no sleeping bags for warmth, they knew they would die if they stayed on the mountain overnight. They needed to get down as quickly as possible. Ernest looked down the slope once more and suggested they slide down it on their bottoms. He knew that the slope could either level out into a snowfield at the bottom or simply drop off the edge of a cliff. Rocks might even be protruding from the snow on the way down. But what choice did they have? "It's a devil of a risk,

I know," Ernest told the others, "but we have to take it. We can't stay up here."

No one said much as they coiled the rope and placed it under them. They sat one behind the other, Ernest in front, Frank at the back, each man's knees wrapped around the man in front of him. Once in position, they all leaned forward and pushed off with their hands. They began rapidly gathering speed. Wind and snow beat against Ernest's face. He didn't know for how long—a minute, two minutes, three minutes—they careened down the mountainside in what felt to him more like flying than sliding. As the slope gradually leveled out, they came to a stop in a soft snowbank. The three men laughed with joy. They had made it to the bottom—alive! They shook hands and clapped each other on the back. Frank estimated that they had dropped two or three thousand feet in altitude and traveled a mile or more down the mountain.

The men walked on a short distance and boiled some more hoosh. By now they had been hiking for sixteen hours. Once they had eaten, Frank checked their position. They set off hiking again in an easterly direction, making their way through an enormous icefield. In the moonlight they could see more mountains ahead that needed to be crossed. By midnight they were at the top of another pass, from which they could see the ocean on the north side of the island glistening in the moonlight. At the bottom of the pass they found themselves on a crevasse-riddled glacier. Because Ernest knew that it was too dangerous to cross it at night, he led them along the edge of the mountain and around the glacier.

By five o'clock in the morning they were ascending another mountain pass, which they reached about six o'clock. From the top of the pass there was still enough moonlight to make out a snowfield spread at the bottom of the mountain. To the east they could see a bay, which Frank believed was Stromness Bay—their destination.

They walked down the mountain and found a sheltered spot to prepare another pot of hoosh. When they had eaten, Ernest asked Frank the time.

"Six fifty-five," the Skipper answered.

"Let's listen for the whaling station whistle at seven. Then we'll know we're in the right spot," Ernest said.

Ernest waited anxiously as the minutes ticked by. They had to be in the right place. If they weren't, he wasn't sure they had the energy to carry on hiking much farther. Then he heard it—the shrill of a distant steam whistle wafting up from the bay below. The three men slapped each other on the back and laughed out loud. As far as Ernest was concerned, it was the sweetest music he had ever heard.

Ernest felt invigorated knowing that a whaling station was below. Since the fuel for the Primus stove was now gone, they left the stove behind and set out again. They still had several miles to cover to reach the station.

Again Ernest led the way. When they reached a steep ice slope, he cut steps for the other two to follow. There was a bay below, but it was Fortuna Bay. Stromness was the next bay over. They climbed up again and made their way farther east before beginning to descend once more. Soon they were staring down onto Stromness Bay. In the distance they could see the Stromness whaling station and two ships anchored in the water.

Ernest decided to follow a stream of snowmelt down a gully toward the bay, but the gully grew narrower as they descended, until the three were walking in water to their knees. Suddenly the stream flowed over a cliff. Ernest peered cautiously over the edge. The water dropped about fifty feet to the ground below and flowed on.

Because none of the three men wanted to walk back upstream to find another route down, they decided to take their chances over the waterfall. They lowered the end of their rope to the ground below. Frank held it while first Ernest, then Tom, slipped down it. When it was the Skipper's turn, he wrapped the end of the rope around some rocks. He placed another rock on top and jumped over the edge of the waterfall, letting the rope slip through his hand and not putting any weight on it until he reached the bottom. Ernest and Tom helped break his fall. The rope held. They were down.

The men headed for the whaling station. As they approached it, Ernest could only imagine how frightening they must appear. They were walking in from the interior of the island where no one had ever been. They were gaunt, exhausted, their clothes tattered and torn, their exposed skin black with soot, grease, and grime, and their hair and beards matted. None of them had taken a bath in months, and they had become used to how they smelled. Ernest's suspicions were confirmed when they walked around the corner of a building and startled two young boys, who looked at the three wild men and ran.

Thirty-six hours after setting out on their trek, they made it to the whaling station manager's house. Ernest stumbled up the steps and knocked on the door. When a man answered it, he asked, "Is Captain Sørlle here?"

"What do you want with him?" the man asked, eying Ernest up and down.

"I know him and wish to see him," Ernest replied.

The man went inside. A minute later Captain Thoralf Sørlle stepped outside.

"Do you know me?" Ernest asked.

"No. Should I?" Captain Sørlle snapped in heavily accented English. "Who are you?"

"I'm Ernest Shackleton." Ernest watched as the burly Norwegian captain's mouth dropped open with surprise.

The captain held out his hand to shake Ernest's. "Come in. Come in," he said. "We thought you were dead!"

"Tell me," Ernest inquired. "When was the war over?"

"It's not over. Millions are being killed. Europe is mad. The world is mad. I will tell you all about it, but first come inside," the captain said.

"I'm afraid we stink," Ernest remarked.

Captain Sørlle chuckled. "That doesn't matter. We're used to smells on a whaling station." With that he led the three men inside. It was the first house Ernest had entered since leaving South Georgia for Antarctica.

Chapter 20

"We Are All Well, Boss"

Inside Captain Sørlle's house, Ernest enjoyed a hot bath. In fact, a bath had never felt so good to him. Layers of dirt and grime dissolved off his body, turning the bath water dark grey. After shaving and putting on the new clothes the station manager supplied, he sat down to a hot, nutritious meal. Afterward he sank onto a soft mattress in a warm room and slept soundly all night.

The next morning Frank accompanied the crew of the *Samson*, a whale catcher, to King Haakon Bay to rescue the three men they had left behind. While they were gone, Ernest and Captain Sørlle talked over coffee served with scones, cakes, and bread. As Ernest drank and ate, the captain told him all he knew of the war. German forces and opposing British, French, and Allied troops were bogged down in trenches in eastern France. The war seemed deadlocked, and the sheer scale of slaughter with no territorial gains to show for it was beyond Captain Sørlle's understanding.

Ernest's mouth dropped open when he learned of the technical advances being used to fight the war. The Germans were using poison gas. Huge metal contraptions called tanks with cannons mounted on them crawled over the ground. Submarines were also being used in the war, as were airplanes. To Ernest, it all sounded like something from the futuristic Jules Verne novels he had read as a boy.

When Captain Sørlle finished describing the state of the war, Ernest told him about some of the ordeal he and his men had been through. The captain listened quietly as Ernest recounted the details of crossing the Southern Ocean in an open boat and trekking across South Georgia.

Afterward Captain Sørlle told Ernest some news that seemed more fantastic to him than the technological advances being used in the war. The captain explained that although there was no telegraph on South Georgia, a ship's captain recently arriving from England had brought word that the badly damaged *Aurora,* the second ship of the Imperial Trans-Antarctic Expedition, had limped into Port Chambers, New Zealand, seven weeks before, on April 2, 1916. Apparently the *Aurora* had been anchored up and was wintering over off Cape Evans in McMurdo Sound when in early May 1915 a severe gale tore the ship from her moorings and carried her out to sea. Like the *Endurance*, the *Aurora* had become stuck in pack ice and drifted northward out of McMurdo Sound into the Ross Sea. Unlike the *Endurance*, the *Aurora* was not crushed by the ice, although she was damaged. On February 12, 1916, after drifting over eighteen hundred miles in pack ice, she had broken free and made her way to New Zealand. More devastating to Ernest was the news that when the *Aurora* was ripped from her mooring, she had left ten men behind on the ice. The men were still there. Now ten more of his men were waiting on the other side of Antarctica to be rescued. Ernest could hardly believe it.

The next day Ernest and Tom sailed over to Husvik whaling station, where the *Southern Sky*, an English steamship with a steel hull used for whaling, was laid up for winter. Ernest hoped to negotiate the use of the vessel to rescue the men from Elephant Island. The ship was made available. Ingvar Thom, a Norwegian captain, volunteered to command her, and a number of whalers stepped forward as crewmen. Then two days after setting out, the *Samson* returned from King Haakon Bay with the three rescued men and the *James Caird*.

When he saw Ernest, Frank explained with a grin that when he landed at King Haakon Bay to retrieve the men, Tim had complained, "We thought the Skipper would have come back to rescue us."

"Well, I'm here, right in front of you," the Skipper had told them. The three men had stared at him in disbelief. It took a few moments for them to decide that the bathed, clean-shaven man in new clothes was really who he said he was.

Ernest chuckled. "I dare say the men on Elephant Island might react the same way when we arrive to rescue them." He was already thinking ahead to the next stage of the long saga that had started out as the Imperial Trans-Antarctic Expedition.

The Norwegian sailors understood the importance of the *James Caird* and insisted she be sent back to England. When the boat was unloaded from the *Samson*, sailors and whalers gathered to watch several sailors lift her and solemnly carry her on their shoulders to the end of the dock. The *James Caird* would be loaded aboard the first ship heading to England. Ernest and the men who had sailed her across the Southern Ocean were deeply touched by the gesture. It was as if the boat were a hero to them as well.

That evening, Captain Thom held a reception aboard his ship in honor of Ernest and the other five men. The captains, seamen, and whalers who gathered in the ship's saloon listened spellbound as Ernest and Frank relayed some of the ordeal they had gone through to make it to Stromness Bay. After hearing the men's story, an old, white-haired sailor came forward to address the group. He spoke in Norwegian, and Captain Sørlle translated. The sailor explained that he had been at sea over forty years and knew the stormy Southern Ocean intimately. Yet in all those years, he had never heard of such a wonderful feat of seamanship as sailing a 22½-foot open boat from Elephant Island to South Georgia. And then the men had crowned *that* success with three of them being the first to trek across the ice and snow and rocky heights of the island's interior. The old sailor said it was an honor to shake hands with Sir Ernest Shackleton and his comrades. "These are men!" he exclaimed. Ernest was moved. He knew that the remark, coming from a member of a great seafaring race like the Norwegians, was a wonderful tribute.

The next morning, Tuesday, May 23, 1916, four days after arriving at Stromness whaling station, Ernest, Frank, and Tom sailed on the *Southern Sky* to rescue the men on Elephant Island. Chippy, John, and Tim stayed behind, awaiting the next ship back to England.

Ernest paced the deck, eager to rescue his men. Three days later and one hundred miles from Elephant Island, the *Southern Sky* encountered ice. The men picked their way through it for another forty miles before the ship could go no farther without the ice tearing her unprotected steel hull open. In frustration, Ernest stood on the bridge as Captain Thom brought the *Southern Sky* about. But instead of returning to South Georgia, Ernest had the ship head for Port Stanley in the Falkland Islands, where there was a telegraph station he could use to find a more suitable vessel.

Arriving in Port Stanley on May 31, Ernest went straight to the telegraph station and sent several messages to England. He was sure that when the messages arrived, they would cause a stir. He imagined that most people in England had given him up for dead, as Captain Sørlle had.

Because no suitable ship was available in the Falklands for a rescue mission, Ernest telegraphed the British Admiralty. He received a telegraph back saying it would be September before a suitable ship made it to Port Stanley. Ernest didn't think the men on Elephant Island could hold out that long. He telegraphed the governments of Argentina, Uruguay, and Chile, asking for a ship. To Ernest's relief, Uruguay offered to send the *Instituto de Pesca No. 1*, a trawler, to Port Stanley from Montevideo. The vessel arrived on Saturday, June 10, and left Port Stanley that night with Ernest, Frank, and Tom aboard.

It was now winter in the Southern Hemisphere, and the sailors encountered bad weather, but the trawler pushed on through rough sea. After three days the peaks of Elephant Island were spotted on the horizon, but the trawler could get no closer than thirty miles to the island because of pack ice. The captain told Ernest they would have to return to Port Stanley.

Back in Port Stanley, Ernest was frantic. The men had been on Elephant Island for two months. Telegraphs arrived from Norway promising a ship for the rescue, and the United States said they might be able to make a ship available. But it would still take months to get a ship to Port Stanley, and Ernest still wasn't sure that the men on the island would survive that long.

From Port Stanley, the three men caught a mail boat to Punta Arenas near the southern tip of Chile, where Ernest hoped he might have more luck securing a rescue boat. An active British association was located there. The members rallied around, raising money and helping Ernest charter the *Emma*, a forty-year-old schooner built of oak. The men departed Punta Arenas on July 12, but more disappointment lay ahead. The men sailed to within one hundred miles of Elephant Island, and then storms and ice forced them to turn back. The weather was so bad that the *Emma* didn't arrive back at Punta Arenas until August 3.

Ernest couldn't believe it. Days had turned to weeks, and now months, and his men were still stranded on Elephant Island. The Chilean government agreed to loan Ernest the *Yelcho*, a small steel tugboat, to make another rescue attempt. The vessel wasn't really suitable for the purpose, but Ernest was desperate. On Friday, August 25, the *Yelcho* set out from Punta Arenas with Ernest and the other two aboard. This time the weather held, and they enjoyed a safe passage south. By evening on August 29, they were sixty miles off Elephant Island. To Ernest's delight, they were still sailing in open water. In fact, it appeared that the wind and current had pushed the pack ice away from the island. Ernest knew that it would eventually return, but right now it opened the hope of rescuing the stranded men.

The boat sailed through the night and by morning was off the northwest point of Elephant Island. Once he had his bearings, Frank navigated their way along the mist-shrouded north coast to the spit where they had left the men over four months before. At 11:40 a.m. on August 30, 1916, the Skipper spotted the camp, almost hidden from view under a layer of snow. The *Yelcho* was about a mile and a half offshore and immediately began steaming toward the beach. Ernest watched as tiny black figures gathered on the shore and waved frantically at them.

Someone lit a bright signal fire on a rocky outcrop at the side of the beach. The *Yelcho* came to a stop, and a rowboat was lowered over the side. Ernest, Tom, and several Chilean sailors headed for shore. As they approached the beach, Ernest recognized Frank Wild standing on a rock. He called out, "Are you all well?"

"We are all well, Boss," came the resounding response from the men on the beach, followed by three cheers.

As soon as the boat touched the beach, Ernest jumped ashore and shook Frank's hand, congratulating him for keeping everyone alive. Because the pack ice could return at any time, there was no time to delay in getting the men off the beach and onto the *Yelcho*. They needed to leave Elephant Island as soon as possible to avoid being trapped. At the top of the beach Ernest could see how the men had fashioned a shelter using the upturned *Dudley Docker* and *Stancomb Wills* and a tarpaulin. He would have loved to have seen inside, but there wasn't time.

Within an hour everyone had been ferried aboard the *Yelcho*, along with the men's diaries and other scant personal items. Leonard Hussey clutched his banjo. Frank Hurley's box of glass photographic plates and various expedition records and logs were also loaded. Once everyone was aboard, the *Yelcho* steamed north away from Elephant Island at top speed. They had beaten the pack ice. Soon the rest of the twenty-two men would be reintroduced to civilization at Punta Arenas.

As they steamed north, Frank Wild told Ernest about the ordeal on Elephant Island. The men had held up reasonably well. Each morning he had told them, "Get your things ready, boys. The Boss may come today." Leonard's banjo playing had helped lift the men's spirits. James McIlroy and Alexander Macklin, the expedition's two doctors, had kept busy tending the men's medical needs, including amputating all the toes on Perce's left foot, which were frostbitten and had become gangrenous. Lewis Rickinson, the *Endurance*'s chief engineer, had suffered a mild heart attack, and navigator Hubert Hudson had had a nervous breakdown. He also had a badly infected abscess on his buttocks, from which the two doctors drained two pints of foul-smelling fluid. Frank admitted that he was glad that Ernest had arrived when he did. There weren't many penguins or seals at this time of year, and the men had less than a week's worth of food supplies left on Elephant Island.

When the *Yelcho* docked in Punta Arenas, Ernest and the rescued men received a rousing welcome. Flags flew and marching bands played and lots of cheering went up as the men came ashore.

The *Endurance* portion of the expedition officially ended on Sunday, October 8, 1916, in Buenos Aires, Argentina. Many of the men were eager to get back to Great Britain to enlist to fight in the war. But for Ernest, nothing was more important than the ten men from the expedition awaiting rescue at Cape Evans in Antarctica. He set sail immediately for New Zealand.

On arrival in New Zealand, Ernest learned that the *Aurora* had been refitted at the expense of the New Zealand and Australian governments. A new crew had been appointed, with John Davis as captain. Ernest had arrived just in time to sail south with the ship.

The *Aurora* sailed from Port Chalmers on December 20, 1916. Three weeks later the ship was in McMurdo Sound. At Cape Evans, as Ernest went ashore and made his way toward the hut, seven men came out to greet him on the ice. They included Ernest Joyce, who had been on the *Nimrod* expedition with Ernest, and Ernest Wild, Frank's brother. The men were haggard, dirty, and weak. Ernest reminded himself that they had spent two years trapped in Antarctica not knowing whether they would ever be rescued. He asked where the other three men were. Ernest was told that Arnold Spencer-Smith, their chaplain and photographer, had died nine months before while returning from laying supply depots. And Captain Aeneas Mackintosh and Victor Hayward had disappeared seven months before while trying to cross from Hut Point to Cape Evans and were presumed dead.

Ernest mounted a search for the two missing men but after a week found no trace of them, and the *Aurora* departed McMurdo Sound and headed north for Wellington, New Zealand. They arrived in Wellington on Friday, February 9, 1917. All the men from the Imperial Trans-Antarctic Expedition who had been trapped on the ice were now rescued. The expedition was officially over.

From New Zealand Ernest traveled to Australia and then headed back to England by way of the United States, where he gave a series of lectures about the ordeal.

Chapter 21

The *Quest*

Ernest arrived back in England in May 1917 after being away two and a half years. None of the fanfare was present that had accompanied his return from the *Nimrod* expedition. Great Britain was preoccupied with the war, and the public looked on the Imperial Trans-Antarctic Expedition as a failure. Ernest headed home to Emily and the family. By now twelve-year-old Raymond was attending Harrow, a boys' boarding school, while ten-year-old Cecily was at Roedean School for girls. "Baby" Edward was now five years old and did not recognize his father. Emily had taken on new interests, becoming involved with the Girl Guides and Boy Scouts. Ernest visited his parents and found them both in poor health. His father was going deaf and had given up his medical practice, since he could no longer hear heartbeats through a stethoscope. His mother was still bedridden, as she had been for years.

Ernest was now forty-three years old, three years beyond the age for being conscripted into the military, and he felt every year of his age. His hair was turning grey, and he was having pain in his chest that he refused to talk to a doctor about, even his father. He called it indigestion, but secretly he feared it might be his heart.

Now that he was home, Ernest began catching up on what had happened to members of the *Endurance*'s crew. Tim McCarthy, who had also been on the *James Caird* voyage, immediately signed up for service in the Royal Navy Reserve upon his return to England. He was assigned to the SS *Narragansett.* Just three weeks after returning from South Georgia, on his first voyage, a German U-boat torpedoed the ship off the south coast of England. Tim and forty-five other sailors lost their lives in the attack. It was hard for Ernest to believe that a man who had survived so many hardships had lost his life so soon after entering the war.

Many other men from the expedition had enlisted in the war effort on their return home. Thomas Orde-Lees had returned to active service with the Royal Marines in November 1916 and now served on the Western Front with the Balloon Corps. Frank Wild had been made a lieutenant in the Royal Naval Volunteer Reserve and was enrolled in a Russian language course. Frank Worsley was an officer on a Q-ship, a specially outfitted merchant vessel designed to damage or destroy German U-boats preying on unarmed merchant ships. Tom Crean returned to the Royal Navy and was promoted to warrant officer. On his return to Hull, Alf Cheetham, the *Endurance*'s third officer, learned that his sixteen-year-old son had drowned while serving on the SS *Adriatic*. Alf enlisted in the war effort and served aboard the SS *Prunelle* as second officer.

Even though he was three years past the age for conscription, Ernest longed to serve his country. However, no one could decide quite where Sir Ernest Shackleton fit in the war effort. Ernest bombarded the War Office with ideas of how and where he could serve. Six months after arriving home, Ernest was sent to a place he least expected—South America. His assignment under the Department of Information was to travel around South America investigating how German propaganda was being used to sway the officially neutral countries. If the Germans were allowed to use ports in South America, they would have a much wider range for their ships and submarines.

In many ways it was a job only Ernest could do. He was well known and well liked in South America and had many contacts in high places who would trust him with information. Before he left, Ernest was summoned to Sandringham House in Norfolk to give a lecture to King George V on the Imperial Trans-Antarctic Expedition. He brought with him a list of men from the *Endurance* whom he hoped the king would award the Polar Medal. Four men were not on the list—those Ernest felt were disloyal to him and did not deserve the medal.

For the next five months Ernest traveled throughout South America keeping his eyes and ears open and relaying his impressions back to the Minister of Information. Then, in March 1918, he was recalled to London. By now the United States had entered the war with large numbers of fresh recruits, but the Germans were still on the offensive in France.

In February 1918, King George V had awarded the Polar Medal to those members of the Imperial Trans-Antarctic Expedition whom Ernest had recommended for the honor. After the medals were awarded, Ernest and a number of the crew got together for dinner to celebrate their achievement. It was wonderful for him to be back among old friends.

Ernest felt that because he and the crew members had been such a strong team on the ice, they should be given an assignment together for the war. The opportunity soon came when the War Department asked Ernest to join the Allied effort to hold back Russia's Red Army. Like many facets of the war, it was sometimes difficult to understand who was fighting whom and why. That had become the case in Russia, where a revolution had begun in October the previous year and still continued. The two main groups fighting for power in the country were the Bolshevik Red Army, who wanted to turn Russia into a Communist state; and the White Army, who wanted the czar, along with a system of capitalism, for the country. The Allies supported the White Army. Ernest's job was to secure a supply line of equipment to the North Russian Expedition, as the Allied intervention force was known. Since the Arctic

Circle ran through northern Russia, temperatures during winter dropped far below freezing and there was lots of snow and ice. Because Ernest knew how to deal with such conditions, he quickly contacted members of his old team to help him. Frank Wild, James McIlroy, Frank Worsley, Leonard Hussey, and Alexander Macklin, from the *Endurance*, Joseph Stenhouse from the *Aurora*, and Eric Marshall from the *Nimrod* expedition all answered the call.

Just as he was leaving for northern Russia, Ernest learned that Alf Cheetham had been killed when the SS *Prunelle* was torpedoed by a German U-boat in the North Sea. Ernest hoped that the same fate didn't await him as he set out on his mission. The team arrived safely in Murmansk, Russia. Ernest was above the Arctic Circle and back in the polar regions in which he thrived. Two weeks after their arrival, on November 11, 1918, the war with Germany was over. But the bloody war for the control of Russia continued. In Murmansk, Ernest and his team kept busy making sure that supplies—clothing, rations, and equipment—got through to the soldiers fighting. Ernest was considered too old to take an active role in the fighting. He stayed in Russia until mid-March 1919, when he returned to England, while other members of the group stayed on to continue fighting. For Ernest, the war was over.

Needing to earn money, Ernest turned again to the speaking circuit. In November 1919, the book he had written about the Imperial Trans-Antarctic Expedition, titled *South*, was published, and it renewed people's interest in him and the expedition. The following month he began a series of lectures at the Philharmonic Hall in London. The series ran until the following Easter, with Ernest speaking and showing a film and photographs of the expedition twice a day, six days a week.

By the time the lecture series had ended, Ernest was thoroughly bored with saying the same thing over and over. He longed for a new adventure, not to be talking about a past one. He set his sights on the North Pole and exploring the Beaufort Sea. No British expedition had yet made it to the North Pole, and Ernest felt that doing so would be a great morale boost to the war-battered country.

In early 1920 he applied to the Royal Geographical Society for support. They approved the expedition but suggested that Ernest approach the Canadian government, since the Beaufort Sea lay above Alaska and Canada's Northwest Territories. The area consisted of about 180,000 square miles of unexplored frozen ocean. Much to Ernest's delight, the Canadian government gave the plan their support, and the largest newspapers in England eagerly agreed to cover the expedition in their publications.

Later that year, Ernest's father died, leaving his mother and two unmarried sisters for him to help support. This made Ernest even more determined to make the expedition a success.

Ernest traveled to Norway, where he bought a sturdy whaling ship and renamed it *Quest*. One of his old Dulwich College school friends, John Quiller Rowett, who had become wealthy, offered to help fund the expedition. The next month Ernest was in Canada planning the expedition specifics and designing the changes he wanted made to the ship. He wanted her to be a thoroughly modern ship and had her outfitted with electricity throughout. Not only did the cabins have electric lights, but also the crow's nest was heated. Heated overalls were available for the men to wear on watch. An odograph, which could automatically trace and chart the ship's route, was installed, along with a wireless set so that *Quest* could be in contact with the outside world at all times. Best of all was the airplane that Ernest was going to take along. He knew that this would be a wonderful aid in navigating through the ice and scouting what lay ahead. He signed up New Zealand pilot Roderick Carr to fly and maintain the plane.

Ernest put out a call for crew members for the expedition. His old team rallied around their leader once more. Frank Wild was second-in-command, and Frank Worsley agreed to captain the *Quest*. Others from the *Endurance,* including the two doctors, Alexander Macklin and James McIlroy, along with Leonard Hussey, Alexander Kerr, Tom McLeod, and Charles Green the cook, signed on. James Dell, a veteran of the *Discovery* expedition twenty years earlier, also joined the crew. Nine other new crew members and even two Boy Scouts had been selected to be part of the epic adventure.

Within days of returning from the planning trip to Canada, Ernest received a telegraph from the Canadian government: the expedition was off. The ruling Union Party feared that helping fund the *Quest* and the expedition might seem frivolous when there were so many returned veterans from the war needing help, especially since the government was facing an upcoming election.

By now the *Quest* was docked on the Thames River in London, with one hundred dogs, an eighteen-man crew, and two Boy Scouts ready to depart, but for where? With the government in Canada no longer welcoming him, Ernest once more turned his eyes south. He decided to make one more voyage to Antarctica, where they would circumnavigate the continent and map about two thousand miles of uncharted coastline.

John Quiller Rowett generously added more money to the expedition's financial pot, and what was officially called the Shackleton-Rowett Expedition got under way. On September 24, 1921, the *Quest* sailed out of Plymouth Sound into the open sea and headed south. That night Ernest wrote in his journal, "At last we are off. Providence is with us even now."

Chapter 22

Star in the Night

They were not far out in the Atlantic Ocean when the *Quest* developed problems. Her engine started knocking, and she sat low in the water, sending waves cascading across her deck, even in good weather. Next the boiler developed a crack. Each separate problem concerned Ernest. Together the problems required immediate action. The *Quest* docked in Lisbon, Portugal, and then Madeira for repairs. The ship then headed for Rio de Janeiro, Brazil, for an engine overhaul.

The overhaul took a month. During that time Ernest struggled with Rio de Janeiro's humid November heat. His shoulders and chest hurt most of the time, but he wouldn't allow either doctor aboard the *Quest* to examine him. Above all, Ernest wanted to go south and did not want to be told to leave the ship for the sake of his health.

On December 18, 1921, the *Quest* was ready to sail again, first for South Georgia to take on fresh supplies, and then to Antarctica. The weather was foul and the sea as rough as any Ernest had encountered. After more than two weeks of battling the ocean, the *Quest* sailed into King Edward Cove and dropped anchor off Grytviken. As he stood on deck and looked around, Ernest recalled the month the *Endurance* had spent anchored in the same spot. He thought of the last time he set foot on South Georgia, of the grueling voyage in the *James Caird,* and the trek across the island to Stromness. As difficult as these had been, Ernest thought of them as part of life's grand adventure. And now another adventure awaited. He was returning south to Antarctica.

At anchor on the calm bay, Ernest promised the crew of the *Quest* that tomorrow they would celebrate Christmas with a delicious dinner since Charles had been unable to prepare one on Christmas Day because of the rough sea. With enough time to go ashore before nightfall, Ernest visited the old whaling station manager and several whalers he knew.

Ernest was back aboard the *Quest* by twilight. He looked up at the sky and saw a single star hovering over the bay. For a moment he was back at Kilkea House in Ireland on his make-believe ship in the fallen tree trunk on the lawn where he had spent many happy times pretending to be a sailor. He smiled to himself and retired for the night. The ship was safe at anchor. Tomorrow would be a good day.

At two o'clock the following morning, January 5, 1922, Ernest awoke with searing pain in his back and chest. He pulled the watchman's bell beside his bunk, and Alexander Macklin came to see what he wanted. Ernest asked for something to dull the pain. The doctor went for his medical kit. He returned and gave Ernest some medication, but it was too late. The Boss died at 3:00 a.m. He was forty-seven years old.

The *Quest*'s two doctors, Alexander Macklin and James McIlroy, performed an autopsy aboard ship and concluded that Sir Ernest Shackleton had died of a heart attack. Ernest's body was dressed and sewn into a canvas bag, which was placed in a coffin for transport home to England. Leonard Hussey accompanied the body aboard a whaler headed for Montevideo, Uruguay, the first stop on the trip home.

Frank Wild, Ernest's ever loyal second-in-command, took over running the *Quest*. He decided that the expedition would go on. That is what the Boss would have wanted.

When the coffin reached Montevideo, a message was waiting from Lady Shackleton. Emily asked that her husband's body be returned to the place he had died and be buried there. She thought it was where he belonged. After a tremendous send-off by the Uruguayans, Ernest's coffin was put aboard the steamer *Woodville*, and Leonard Hussey returned with it to Grytviken on South Georgia island.

On March 5, 1922, below the towering peaks that Ernest had struggled over to save his men, a funeral service was held in the Lutheran church.

Afterward, the body of Ernest Shackleton was buried in the tiny Grytviken cemetery. The whalers who buried him faced him toward the south. It seemed the right thing to do.

Bibliography

Alexander, Caroline. *The* Endurance: *Shackleton's Legendary Antarctic Expedition.* New York: Alfred A. Knopf, 1998.

Fisher, Margery, and James Fisher. *Shackleton.* London: James Barrie Books, 1957.

Huntford, Roland. *Shackleton.* New York: Carroll and Graf, 1998.

Lansing, Alfred. *Endurance: Shackleton's Incredible Voyage.* New York: Carroll and Graf, 1986.

Shackleton, Ernest. *South: The Last Antarctic Expedition of Shackleton and the* Endurance. New York: Lyons, 1998.

Shackleton, Jonathan, and John MacKenna. *Shackleton: An Irishman in Antarctica.* Dublin: Lilliput, 2002.

Smith, Michael. *Shackleton: By Endurance We Conquer.* London: Oneworld, 2014.

About the Authors

Janet and Geoff Benge are a husband and wife writing team with more than thirty years of writing experience. Janet is a former elementary school teacher. Geoff holds a degree in history. Together they have a passion to make history come alive for a new generation of readers.

Originally from New Zealand, the Benges make their home in the Orlando, Florida, area.

Heroes of History are available in paperback, e-book, and audiobook formats, with more coming soon! Unit Study Curriculum Guides are available for many biographies.

www.HeroesThenAndNow.com

Also from Janet and Geoff Benge…

More adventure-filled biographies for ages 10 to 100!

Christian Heroes: Then and Now

Gladys Aylward: The Adventure of a Lifetime • 978-1-57658-019-6
Nate Saint: On a Wing and a Prayer • 978-1-57658-017-2
Hudson Taylor: Deep in the Heart of China • 978-1-57658-016-5
Amy Carmichael: Rescuer of Precious Gems • 978-1-57658-018-9
Eric Liddell: Something Greater Than Gold • 978-1-57658-137-7
Corrie ten Boom: Keeper of the Angels' Den • 978-1-57658-136-0
William Carey: Obliged to Go • 978-1-57658-147-6
George Müller: Guardian of Bristol's Orphans • 978-1-57658-145-2
Jim Elliot: One Great Purpose • 978-1-57658-146-9
Mary Slessor: Forward into Calabar • 978-1-57658-148-3
David Livingstone: Africa's Trailblazer • 978-1-57658-153-7
Betty Greene: Wings to Serve • 978-1-57658-152-0
Adoniram Judson: Bound for Burma • 978-1-57658-161-2
Cameron Townsend: Good News in Every Language • 978-1-57658-164-3
Jonathan Goforth: An Open Door in China • 978-1-57658-174-2
Lottie Moon: Giving Her All for China • 978-1-57658-188-9
John Williams: Messenger of Peace • 978-1-57658-256-5
William Booth: Soup, Soap, and Salvation • 978-1-57658-258-9
Rowland Bingham: Into Africa's Interior • 978-1-57658-282-4
Ida Scudder: Healing Bodies, Touching Hearts • 978-1-57658-285-5
Wilfred Grenfell: Fisher of Men • 978-1-57658-292-3
Lillian Trasher: The Greatest Wonder in Egypt • 978-1-57658-305-0
Loren Cunningham: Into All the World • 978-1-57658-199-5
Florence Young: Mission Accomplished • 978-1-57658-313-5
Sundar Singh: Footprints Over the Mountains • 978-1-57658-318-0
C.T. Studd: No Retreat • 978-1-57658-288-6
Rachel Saint: A Star in the Jungle • 978-1-57658-337-1
Brother Andrew: God's Secret Agent • 978-1-57658-355-5
Clarence Jones: Mr. Radio • 978-1-57658-343-2
Count Zinzendorf: Firstfruit • 978-1-57658-262-6
John Wesley: The World His Parish • 978-1-57658-382-1
C. S. Lewis: Master Storyteller • 978-1-57658-385-2
David Bussau: Facing the World Head-on • 978-1-57658-415-6
Jacob DeShazer: Forgive Your Enemies • 978-1-57658-475-0
Isobel Kuhn: On the Roof of the World • 978-1-57658-497-2
Elisabeth Elliot: Joyful Surrender • 978-1-57658-513-9
D. L. Moody: Bringing Souls to Christ • 978-1-57658-552-8
Paul Brand: Helping Hands • 978-1-57658-536-8
Dietrich Bonhoeffer: In the Midst of Wickedness • 978-1-57658-713-3
Francis Asbury: Circuit Rider • 978-1-57658-737-9
Samuel Zwemer: The Burden of Arabia • 978-1-57658-738-6

Klaus-Dieter John: Hope in the Land of the Incas • 978-1-57658-826-2
Mildred Cable: Through the Jade Gate • 978-1-57658-886-4
John Flynn: Into the Never Never • 978-1-57658-898-7
Richard Wurmbrand: Love Your Enemies • 978-1-57658-987-8
Charles Mulli: We Are Family • 978-1-57658-894-9
John Newton: Change of Heart • 978-1-57658-909-0
Helen Roseveare: Mama Luka • 978-1-57658-910-6
Norman Grubb: Mission Builder • 978-1-57658-915-1
Albert Schweitzer • 978-1-57658-961-8

Heroes of History

George Washington Carver: From Slave to Scientist • 978-1-883002-78-7
Abraham Lincoln: A New Birth of Freedom • 978-1-883002-79-4
Meriwether Lewis: Off the Edge of the Map • 978-1-883002-80-0
George Washington: True Patriot • 978-1-883002-81-7
William Penn: Liberty and Justice for All • 978-1-883002-82-4
Harriet Tubman: Freedombound • 978-1-883002-90-9
John Adams: Independence Forever • 978-1-883002-50-3
Clara Barton: Courage under Fire • 978-1-883002-51-0
Daniel Boone: Frontiersman • 978-1-932096-09-5
Theodore Roosevelt: An American Original • 978-1-932096-10-1
Douglas MacArthur: What Greater Honor • 978-1-932096-15-6
Benjamin Franklin: Live Wire • 978-1-932096-14-9
Christopher Columbus: Across the Ocean Sea • 978-1-932096-23-1
Laura Ingalls Wilder: A Storybook Life • 978-1-932096-32-3
Orville Wright: The Flyer • 978-1-932096-34-7
Captain John Smith: A Foothold in the New World • 978-1-932096-36-1
Thomas Edison: Inspiration and Hard Work • 978-1-932096-37-8
Alan Shepard: Higher and Faster • 978-1-932096-41-5
Ronald Reagan: Destiny at His Side • 978-1-932096-65-1
Davy Crockett: Ever Westward • 978-1-932096-67-5
Milton Hershey: More Than Chocolate • 978-1-932096-82-8
Billy Graham: America's Pastor • 978-1-62486-024-9
Ben Carson: A Chance at Life • 978-1-62486-034-8
Louis Zamperini: Redemption • 978-1-62486-049-2
Elizabeth Fry: Angel of Newgate • 978-1-62486-064-5
William Wilberforce: Take Up the Fight • 978-1-62486-057-7
William Bradford: Plymouth's Rock • 978-1-62486-092-8
Ernest Shackleton: Going South • 978-1-62486-093-5
Benjamin Rush: The Common Good • 978-1-62486-123-9
Dwight Eisenhower: Supreme Commander • 978-1-62486-142-0
Frederick Douglass: The Right to Dignity • 978-1-62486-151-2
Winston Chruchill: Resolute • 978-1-62486-153-6

Samuel Zwemer: The Burden of Arabia • 978-1-57658-738-6
Klaus-Dieter John: Hope in the Land of the Incas • 978-1-57658-826-2
Mildred Cable: Through the Jade Gate • 978-157658-886-4
John Flynn: Into the Never Never • 978-1-57658-898-7
Charles Mulli: We Are Family • 978-1-57658-894-9
Richard Wurmbrand: Love Your Enemies • 978-1-57658-987-8

Available in paperback, e-book, and audiobook formats.
Unit Study Curriculum Guides are available for many biographies.
www.HeroesThenAndNow.com